Hoping you're
up + Running in
No time.

"Not only in running, but in much of life, is a
sense of balance and proportion necessary"

-Clarence DeMar

MARATHON

THE AUTOBIOGRAPHY OF
CLARENCE DEMAR

"I just run because I like to run"

-Clarence DeMar
(1888-1958)

Clarence DeMar's
Top Boston Marathon Finishes

Year	Place	Time	Age
1910	2nd	2:29:52	21
1911	1st	2:21:39	22
1917	3rd	2:31:05	28
1922	1st	2:18:10	33
1923	1st	2:23:47	34
1924	1st	2:29:40	35
1925	2nd	2:39:34	36
1926	3rd	2:32:15	37
1927	1st	2:40:22	38
1928	1st	2:37:07	39
1930	1st	2:34:48	41

Additional Stats

- 7-Time Winner of the Boston Marathon*

- Oldest Winner of Boston Marathon *(Age 41)* *

- 33 Boston Marathon finishes *(1910-1954)*

- 3-Time U.S. Olympian- *1912, 1924 (bronze), 1928*

- Oldest Olympic medalist in the marathon event. *(Age 36)**

*Indicates unbroken record as of
September 2016*

MARATHON
The Autobiography of Clarence DeMar
By Clarence DeMar

First published in 1937 by Stephen Daye Press
©1981 The New England Press, Inc
© 1992 by Cedarwinds Publishing Company

© 2016 Driscoll & Co Publishing
Massachusetts, USA

Library of Congress Cataloging in Publication Data
DeMar, Clarence H.
MARATHON

ISBN 978-1-48358-074-6

Photos, including cover photo, Courtesy of Boston Public Library,
Leslie Jones Collection

Cover and back layout by Hudd Byard.
Interior layout by J. Driscoll

ACKNOWLEDGEMENTS

The rebirth of Clarence DeMar's *Marathon* would not have been possible without the following people. Many thanks to:

Amby Burfoot, Hudd Byard, Dr. Paul Thompson M.D., Devyn Giannetti, The Arnold Family, The Meadows Family, Lily Mcadows, Jack E. Driscoll, Jason Brown, Peter, Lauren & Jennifer Driscoll, John Wayno, Julia Lee Aquadro, Marc Davis & the Boston Athletic Association, New England Press, Virginia Adams, Jason Jones, Emily Azadnia, Alan Stroshine & everybody at the annual Clarence DeMar Marathon in Keene, NH.

Special thanks to photographer Leslie Jones for capturing years of incredible photos of Clarence DeMar and the Boston Marathon. Many thanks to Leslie's grandson Bob Cullum and family for making the use of these photos possible, and to Tom Blake, Aaron Schmidt & the folks at the Boston Public Library for digitizing and cataloging this historical collection of 40,000 photos.

To view the Leslie Jones Collection visit:
LeslieJonesPhotography.com

CONTENTS

FOREWORD

by Amby Burfoot
1968 Boston Marathon winner
Editor at Large, Runner's World Magazine

Every serious marathoner should own a copy of this book, Clarence DeMar's autobiography, because he was the first serious marathoner. Numero uno. And the life and lessons he describes in these pages still have much to teach us today. That's why I am so excited to see the birth of this new edition of DeMar's timeless story.

DeMar didn't just win seven Boston Marathons--three more than any other multi-Boston winner. He didn't just run in three Olympic Marathons, and compete in long distance races from 1909 to 1957. In addition, he was the first to approach long-distance running in a studious, even scientific manner. He considered all aspects of the high-performance lifestyle from training to diet to sleep as important ingredients in the marathoner's goal of optimal performance.

If my readings into the history of the Harvard Fatigue Laboratory are correct, DeMar was also the first person to run on a treadmill. In the 1920s physiologists at Harvard used military men as their typical subjects, measuring heart rate, oxygen consumption and other physical responses as the soldiers carried heavy packs while walking on the newfangled treadmills. One of the scientists thought to ask DeMar into the Lab for similar tests, since he was easily the most famous marathoner of that era. He agreed, and followed their instructions for awhile. But then, he said, more or less: "This walking is too easy. Can I try running on your treadmill?"

History doesn't record this as the birth of a huge new industry--indoor gyms and health clubs--but I think it might have been.

I was a teenager when I first heard of DeMar. A recent convert from basketball and baseball to cross-country running at Robert Fitch High School in Groton, Connecticut, I fell under the spell of John J. Kelley--the Fitch cross-country coach, and much more. Kelley was also a Boston Marathon winner, two-time Olympic marathoner, and Renaissance man without equal.

My enthusiasm for Kelley and running knew no bounds, so I read everything I could get my hands on--not much in the early 1960s--about the Boston Marathon. That led inevitably to DeMar's autobiography, which mesmerized me, since I had never encountered so much marathon knowledge between two covers. Several decades later, at a yard sale, I stumbled upon an autographed copy. It became one of my most prized running possessions.

I was most impressed by DeMar's steady character and his dedication to an intense training program. The two seemed closely intertwined. I was surprised to read that DeMar had reached a mega-mileage weekly training amount that I thought my friends and I had invented in the 1960s. Not so! "In getting ready for the race the most important thing is to do a lot of practice," DeMar wrote before I was born. "The amount and speed may vary with individuals, but a great deal must be done. I averaged one hundred miles per week for two months before April 19."

I drew a simple, powerful message from DeMar's life-- one that I used in my own, particularly in my running. Before long, I learned that others had more running talent than I. Perhaps that was why they so often lost sight of the target, and frittered away their gifts. I chose a different path, more like DeMar's, and maintained a narrow, sharp focus on the big goal--winning Boston.

I'm not recommending the single-track life. Life is meant to be rich and varied. But certainly there's a time and a place for extreme concentration. That's what DeMar did. That's what I tried to emulate, and it worked.

Let me tell you another DeMar-inspired story. My friend Paul Thompson, M.D., is one of the world's leading sports cardiologists. Runners and other serious exercisers from around the country fly to Hartford Hospital to seek his counsel. Occasionally, he outright saves someone's life; more often, he explains how an aging man or woman can continue to exercise intelligently while respecting whatever heart problem might have developed. I can't imagine anyone doing more important work than the best doctors among us, and Paul is one of them.

Paul was a young teen living outside Boston when he first began hearing DeMar stories from his Baptist minister father. His father appreciated DeMar's commitment to sports, church, Sunday school, and the pious life. Indeed, DeMar once visited Paul's father's Sunday school class. This made a strong impression. Years later, Paul's father received a copy of DeMar's autobiography in partial payment for officiating at the funeral of a Boston sportswriter. He also took his son (Paul) to see his first Boston Marathon in the early 1960s.

Paul understood his father's reverence for DeMar, and also found himself drawn to the marathon. Competitive by nature but small of stature, Paul didn't excel in any of the mainstream sports. So he tried running, and soon found that it matched his talents and his work ethic. Eventually, Paul qualified for the 1972 U.S. Olympic Marathon Trials, running a 2:28 marathon, and completed the Boston Marathon 29 times.

Another important thread links Clarence DeMar and Paul Thompson. After DeMar died of stomach cancer in 1958 at age 70, several research cardiologists convinced his wife that an autopsy of his heart could make an important contribution to medical science.

The results, published by famed cardiologist Paul Dudley White (who treated President Dwight D. Eisenhower when he had a heart attack white in office), appeared in a famous New England Journal of Medicine issue in 1961. The paper revealed that DeMar had some blockage in his coronary arteries, but that these arteries were "two to three times the normal diameter" for a man his size. This was the first clinical evidence that endurance exercise, previously thought to overly stress the heart, in fact helped the heart and cardiovascular system grow stronger and healthier

Thompson has pursued this theme throughout his medical career, publishing many important papers showing a link between exercise, heart health, and longevity. "Sixty years after DeMar's death, my research and countless other studies continue to show the benefits of living a life like DeMar's--one characterized by endurance exercise, healthy eating, and a 'balanced' life," notes Thompson.

Like all aging runners, DeMar wondered how each decade would affect his life and running performances. He knew he would get slower, but saw no reason to put artificial limits on himself. Instead, he figured that an optimistic outlook was the best approach. The results were outstanding. "Since I was forty and definitely slipping," he wrote, "I have won seven full marathons, got second six times, and third four times; a total of seventeen times within the first three places. I'm wondering what I can do after I'm fifty!

This is why DeMar remains important and pertinent today. In survey after survey, runners proclaim their intent to remain fit for life. DeMar was the first to follow this path, and remains an important touchstone. Readers will be struck by how little has changed in 100 years. What DeMar studied, preached, and lived nearly a century ago is very close to the road many of us are on today.

He was indeed "Mr. DeMarathon." More than that, Clarence DeMar and his story remain a guiding light.

-Amby Burfoot
2016

Clarence DeMar (1910)

Chapter 1
Background for Running

An article in a Cincinnati paper once stated that I could run down a jack-rabbit when I was a boy on Indian Hill, near that city. This was hardly a fact. As a boy I was about the slowest moving youngster in school. I did enter quite a few Fourth of July and Sunday School picnic races, but I never made much of a showing. Once, at the age of fourteen, I did fairly well in a mile race for school-boys. But whatever success I have had at marathoning could not have been foretold from boyhood victories.

I can see some evidences, however, of a background for my becoming a distance runner. When I first started school at the age of seven at Madisonville, Ohio, I had over a mile to go. Even then I found it much more pleasant to dog-trot than to walk. Only I was somewhat ashamed or self-conscious when somebody noticed my method of getting places and said, "Say, sonny, don't you ever walk!"

A little later I had reason to do a lot of walking. My father died and it was necessary for me to help my mother with five smaller brothers and sisters. So I sold things like pins, needles, thread, and soap around the neighboring towns and country. Usually I walked ten or twenty miles when on one of these trips. Of course I frequently got a lift when a horse and buggy came along the country road.

In May, 1936, while out near Cincinnati for the national 50,000 meter walk, I called on several of my relatives who remembered my days of walking around the neighboring towns nearly forty years ago. I might add that the DeMars have always been a rather rugged family. There are thirteen brothers and sisters of my father still living. While none of my numerous uncles and cousins has ever taken up distance running, a team of DeMars once played the Cincinnati Reds in an exhibition game, and were defeated by the close score of 2 to 1.

When I was ten years old, my mother brought us east to live in Warwick, Massachusetts. I continued my practice of walking around the neighborhood selling things. I also did considerable hiking through the woods and around Mount Grace. From the top of the mountain I could see parts of Keene, New Hampshire, but I little supposed that I would spend several years there, a generation later, as a teacher. During our winter at Warwick I skated so much on crusted snow that my ankle became infected and I nearly lost my foot

Although my mother had free house-rent in Warwick (since one of her relatives owned the place), we could hardly make a living. So we broke up housekeeping and separated. I was placed in a home called the Farm School, now the Farm and Trades School, on Thompson's Island in Boston Harbor. My wandering, carefree spirit was cramped by the bounds and rules. I became known as a good student, but very poor at anything else. The only running I did, except for the mile race, which I've already mentioned, was once when several of us tried to run away. Our "running" was done by swimming and by pushing a boat, as the oars were locked up. We aimed to land at Savin Hill, something over a mile away. However, the water was very cold (all my career I've had more success with heat than with cold) and with the aid of the Life Saving Station we were captured and put in the deepest disgrace for several months. I especially recall that in holding us up to ridicule and shame, the Superintendent mentioned my swimming with a peculiar kick, which he called a "twin screw propeller on a Chinese junk." Later in life I was to have my foot and leg motion again ridiculed, this time by athletic coaches. But this swim was the only time it failed to get me there eventually.

The failure of the effort to escape caused me to crawl into my shell tighter than ever and take to story books and study. Finally, the Superintendent decreed that I should walk a mile or so to the south end of the island every noon to inspect a piece of apparatus. He was very sure that I needed the exercise. When graduation came and he presented me with my grammar school diploma, the Superintendent rather doubtfully expressed the hope that I would have the health and strength to accomplish things in life.

Finally, at the age of sixteen, they let me leave the island and go to work for a fruit farmer at South Hero, Vermont. This was hard work and demanded a lot of endurance. I am sure that it was much more fatiguing to pitch hay or cut corn all day than to run a marathon for a quarter of a day. While there I grew stronger, got some education at Maple Lawn Academy, and saved some money out of my ten to twenty dollars a month.

Like most boys, I had always admired athletes and dreamed of becoming one sometime. At times I fancied myself as a great football player, possibly one who could be called back to drop-kick in emergencies. How that ball would gracefully sail through the goal posts! Then there were times when I thought I might become a good boxer and win the World's Championship. But the two or three times that I put on the gloves were disastrous. Possibly baseball, then. If I could only get a hard hit home, that ball would fly. But whenever I swung I missed.

After going on to the farm, I had less time to dream. I worked and studied long hours and lived rather by myself. Then I entered the University of Vermont and was thrown into the midst of all the glamour of college athletics. During those first months on the campus if one of the athletic heroes (we had such names as Ray Collins, Larry Gardner of baseball fame, Merrill on the track and Pierce in Football) even spoke to me I was thrilled.

I had little expectation of doing anything in athletics so I kept plodding along, doing well in my studies and paying my way by chores at the experiment farm, working in print shops, and beating rugs. In dog trotting from one job to another and beating rugs I got plenty of exercise. In fact I used this as an excuse to be let off from gym classes, which I always hated. The alibi worked and I passed physical education without attending classes.

With all my admiration for athletic success and the pleasure I got from glancing at scores in the papers, I seldom went to games. I guess I have never been bitten by the bug of "Spectatoritis." In that respect I am something like Frank Zuna, who wouldn't watch the Olympic Games while a member of the team in 1924. But I always have been bitten by the desire to excel in some form of athletics, and to enjoy the pleasures of actual competition.

Chapter 2
I Take Up Running

The first time my daydreams ever turned to distance running was during my sophomore year at the University of Vermont. It was during the winter of 1908-09 when I had a job delivering small samples of milk each morning from the experiment station to the State Hygiene Laboratory down town. It was less than a mile each way and I always ran, partly to save time and partly to keep warm.

One morning the thought came to me that I could run a marathon, and perhaps go abroad to represent my country. Because newspapers, except the Transcript, had been unavailable at Thompson's Island and I hadn't had time to read them since, the whole marathon idea was hazy to me, but I was quite sure there was such a thing and I thought I could do it,

It was not until my third year at college that I really began to run as an athlete. This is the way it started. From a sense of loyalty I usually went to the college smokers even if I never learned how to smoke then, or since. And I always took to heart the remarks of athletes who spoke to encourage more participation in athletics. Professor Stetson, of the German department, also related his theory that there was some sport in which every man could become a champion. There were lots of kinds of men and lots of sports. If each one would look around, he could find something in which to become a champion.

I decided to try cross-country. I'd never tried that, and candidates were to report the next day. I was there. Personally, I was a little embarrassed to run around in what looked like B.V.D.'s, but with a whole group dressed the same way it was not so bad. That was before the days of sunbaths, Vitamin D and shirtless P.W.A. workers.

At that first trial, the cross-country captain, Stevens, kept yelling at me, "Run on your toes, on your toes!"

I was so used to walking that the heel would hit first and I couldn't get the idea of running by hitting the toes first and then coming back on the heels. I tried to dance along on my toes without the heels touching! Eventually within that year I learned how to run on my toes. Still I have never run that way more than one third of the time. It is a convenient way to run if one has blisters on his heels and it seems to me a trifle faster, but it is more fatiguing. The Finns, I'm told, and have partially verified by observation, all run flat-footed except Ritola, who learned to run in the United States. My whole attitude is that whether one shall run on his heels or his toes is hardly worth discussing. The main thing in distance running is endurance and the ability to get there as quickly as possible.

After a week or two of practice I went into the interclass cross-country race of four miles and came in fourth. The following week in a meet with Union College I came in fourth, beating the Captain Stevens who had told me how to run.

The exhilaration of having made good in a college sport thrilled me. I had almost won my "V," since those were awarded to the first three. The exhilaration of which I speak showed that night at the Alpha Zeta fraternity meeting, for as one brother remarked about me, "He has talked a blue streak all night." A question so often asked at athletic gatherings, "How do you feel after one of those races?" has always been answered by reference to that night, "Very much waked up and exhilarated."

Soon after this, in the middle of the term, I left college and went to live with my mother and one brother and sister in Melrose, Mass. I was now twenty-one and legally able to help support my mother. I continued to live in Melrose at home for twenty years and work as a printer in neighboring cities and Boston.

From the first I decided that whatever else I might do I would be a marathon runner. I ran at the leisurely speed of seven or eight miles per hour, to and from work, usually carrying a dry undershirt. I also bought a small Spaulding book about distance running for ten cents, and studied it carefully. I felt that I could absorb the instruction I needed better from reading than from a coach, since I could cogitate each problem and reach a decision without prejudice. Also, I could make sure I understood the theory before trying to put it into practice. My experience with coaches and would-be coaches in distance running is that they try to tell me something when I'm very tense and excited from running and I misunderstand them and get rattled. While reading and studying this little book I greatly admired Shrub, Longboat, Mahoney, Forshaw and Hatch, but felt a serene confidence that I could eventually do as well as any of them on a full marathon. And I had never run over eight or ten miles in my life!

When Christmas came in 1909, I had a holiday from work and decided to try the full distance to see whether I could do it I ran up through Reading to a part of Andover where a road sign said "Boston 20 miles," and back to Melrose which is seven miles from Boston, I did the 26 miles in about three hours without much exertion and so felt very confident. All winter, regardless of weather, I kept up my running, either to or from work, or both. This made from seven to fourteen miles per day. Frequently the men in the shops showed an interest in my way of travel. Now and then one would advise me of the danger to heart and health. Once a man in the street offered me a dime for carfare; and again while passing through West Everett someone yelled insistently "Hey! Hey! You running?" I stopped. Then he said, "A year from now you'll be dead, running like that." Twenty-seven years have passed by and the dire prophecy is unfulfilled.

On February 22, 1910, there was a 10-mile handicap race held by the Old Armory Athletic Association from Boston to Chestnut Hill and back 1 entered and received a start of 5:15 over a runner named Robinson of Brookline Gym, who was at scratch. The race was held in a rain and sleet storm. I wore an extra blue shirt over my running jersey and many old timers still speak of remembering my first open race. I won with a fair margin over Festus Madden of South Boston and I believe I also had about the second best time. Of course I was much thrilled and excited to see my name and picture in the Boston papers. In later years I became annoyed with so much publicity, however, and was inclined to agree with the man who said, "The trick nowadays is to keep your name and picture out of the papers; it is so common to get in!"

Immediately after this race McGrath cut my handicap to 2:15 and from 1910 to 1935 it stayed at 2 or 2:15. The scratch men changed several times, but my relative ability at ten miles was constant for twenty-five years.

For winning this Armory race my prize was a silver tea set. My mother and sister were delighted with it and while they had never exactly opposed my running this made them more favorable to it. My sister said she had once thought the men who finished the marathon came in all covered with blood, but she revised her opinion when she saw me intact!

After this victory I aimed for the big marathon two months later. I ran several 10-mile races with mediocre results, owing to my low handicap. I recall, for instance, getting ninth in the Cathedral race, which is still held just prior to the marathon. Since there were eight place prizes in those days I was already getting minor disappointments along with the glamour of success.

On April 19, 1910, there was a large field of over two hundred entered for the Boston Athletic Association, or B.A.A.[1] Marathon, as it was called. This list decreased to under seventy-five in succeeding years, but finally rose to a higher number in 1928 and afterwards. I had trained by running leisurely with my clothes on, my only speed work being 10-mile races. Several times I had been out fifteen or twenty miles instead of the usual seven to or from work. As usual I was quite confident of doing well, but uncertain as to how well. The day was fairly hot, so anyone was liable to misjudge the pace.

After we got started I kept a vision of the distance before me and was continually gauging my strength accordingly. This is a sort of subconscious process that takes concentration but always works, barring accidents like the loss of confidence, a gambling spirit, or mild sunstroke. At that time the course was the short one from Ashland, about twenty-four miles. Many of the runners were more developed at ten miles than I, and some were not gauging the pace as carefully, so at Wellesley I was seven minutes back of the leaders. As we passed Woodlawn and began to climb the Newton hills I closed in some and passed a couple of chaps who were badly wilted. Finally, I got up into third place and after a hard battle with James J. Corkey of Toronto, clinched second. One paper said I ran "as if my head were held by a check." I never was a graceful runner, but then, I never have thought an athletic event should be a beauty show! Coming down Commonwealth Avenue just before the turn into Exeter Street I got a glimpse of Freddy Cameron, the winner. This was the first I had seen of him since the start. Cameron won in 2:28 and I was second in 2:29. I did about the same time as Caffrey in his record run of 1901, a mark which had since been displaced by Longboat in 1907.

---

[1] The Boston Marathon was once more commonly referred to as the B.A.A. Marathon.

The North Dorchester Athletic Association, whose colors I wore, and the men in Griffith-Stillings on Congress Street, where I was working, both felt that I had done very well. One printer said he had watched the race and was amused at the number of handlers and sponges some of the crack racers had. "But," he said, "you just ran right past them without ceremony." Probably it will be clear to most people that I consider handlers, spongers, and exhorters a great handicap, anyhow. But both in the shop and at the club I got plenty of cautions that one or two of these marathons were all a man should do in a lifetime.

Early in May I ran a 10-mile handicap race conducted by the "Y" in Lynn. I finished tenth, and several volunteered the information that no runner was ever the same after he had run a marathon, It was suggested that I must always expect to finish way back in the pack of every race after I had once run a full marathon.

During the summer of 1910 I recall running a number of races with varying success. I placed second in a 10-mile scratch race at Haverhill, Mass, on July fourth (the Jeffries-Johnson day). This race was won by Mahoney of Worcester, the New England 10-mile champion for that year. Jimmie Henigan, not yet the great 10-miler he was to become, was third or fourth. I received a gold Howard watch, and its guarantee of twenty years is already outdone.

Early in August I went out to Worcester for a 10-mile scratch race on a half-mile track. The first prize was a twenty-five dollar suit of clothes. This prize was, and is, contrary to A.A.U. rules since clothes cannot be engraved! But before the days of super highways, Worcester was way out in the "sticks" and Mr. Facey, of Cambridge, the A.A.U. secretary-treasurer, was not apt to hear about any violation of rules so far away. As usual I very much needed some new clothes and tried hard to win this suit. But with runners like Tom Lilly, Jimmie Henigan and others, the best I could do that day was fifth.

16

That just gave me a medal. When I brought it home, my mother remarked that a medal was nicer than a cup since it didn't take up so much room! Incidentally, the suit was won by "Honey" Lucas of Fall River. "Honey" has since raised a litter of young ones equal in numbers to that of Jim Henigan or "Pep" Clark, the walker, but he is still competing and often refers to that race. He says that no one will believe that he once beat Henigan and DeMar in the same day. And he says further that the suit was too big for him, and as they wouldn't exchange it he had to sell it at a loss!

But before this happened a couple of athletic fans named Colclough of Malden, and Jordan of Boston, had approached me about letting them help me get into shape to go down to Nova Scotia to run Freddy Cameron, the BAA winner. They had said a great deal about my possibilities and what they could do to help. They talked about eating plenty of meat, getting a long stride, taking breathing exercises and having the "guts" to fight to the finish. Doubtful, but willing to experiment, I accepted their care and guidance for a month or so. They had some of the professional coach's arrogance at times, which I much resented but put up with for experimental reasons. For instance, I remember one bawling out: "Get up off the ground there, you'll catch cold." That stuff may be all right for thick-skinned football players, but will antagonize anyone with any sensitivity. But these fellows aimed to be thorough and do their best for me and so took me to be examined by an old doctor in Roxbury. He told me that I had a slight heart murmur and should not run more than a year or two. I asked him how I'd first notice anything wrong with my heart, and he said that in a few years I'd feel weak, going up and down stairs. I've been looking for these symptoms for over a quarter of a century! In less than two years I heard that the old doctor had died of heart failure himself, so I've often wondered if he wasn't listening to his own heart by mistake.

Colclough and Jordan arranged for the trip to Amherst, Nova Scotia, and of course accompanied me.

They may have had plenty of expense money for their own passage, but they protected my amateur attitude very well by letting me buy my own souvenirs and lose ten days' pay.

Anyhow we all had a good trip. They gave me pep talks, and gossiped with Tom Trenholm, Cameron's coach. As I would now expect, I finished in the rut in both the ten and fifteen-mile races against such finished runners as Cameron, Hackett, and Robinson. That gave me a pretext to tell the would-be coaches that the athletic experiment was over and if they wanted to go in for running they should be contestants, not coaches.

My next full marathon was the Brockton Fair race in the fall of 1910. Billy Hackett, the 1909 winner, was the favorite. During the summer I had acquired some speed, which I used in the excitement of the early stages of this marathon to my later grief. I took the lead from Harrop of Fall River at Mattapan and increased this to nearly a mile at Randolph. But in the last miles both Hackett and Piggott passed me; I finished third and very tired.

Then there was the New England 10-mile championship at Waltham, Mass., on Thanksgiving Day. In this race I finished second to Cooke of Brookline with the ever-threatening Jimmie Henigan third. This second in a New England Championship was the best I did towards a sectional gold medal until I got the New England marathon in 1934. Meanwhile I had won several national championships but it took a quarter of a century to win the honor in my own section!

To complete my first year of racing I ran a 20-mile indoor relay race in the Charlestown armory with Al Upham, then of Dorchester, now of San Diego, California, as my partner. In these races, the runners relieve each other at will, making the contest a series of dashes and very grueling. Among the other teams were Bob Fowler and Joe Silva, Hayden and Neller of New York, and Henigan and Hackett. On the first lap my partner got a slight lead, which I took, but being inexperienced in indoor running I slipped on the second corner and made a general spill and heap. Once, in the middle of the race, Upham let me do several laps beyond my quota. Afterwards he said, "You were doing so well I just let you keep on." We did finally get second, beating out the New York team of Hayden and Sammy Neller, with Bob Fowler and Joe Silva winning.

All this running in 1910 made a good background for success in 1911.

Chapter 3
1911

This was the year that I would have graduated from the University of Vermont if I had stayed. But instead it marks my introduction to victory in the big Boston Marathon. I don't say this in comparison but merely for the sake of the record.

As a preliminary, I entered the annual Armory A.A. ten-mile race on Washington's birthday, which I had won the year before. Over the frozen snow I managed to get sixth from a low mark and also won the time prize. Entering this race with a marathoner's caution not to tire himself with too much competition, nor to unsettle his pace, I passed up the Cathedral run and entered the B.A.A. next.

I had worked hard in practice covering nearly a hundred miles per week for a couple of months with several twenty-mile jaunts, besides my regular runs to and from work. One of the first of many physical difficulties I have met before races annoyed me this time. My right knee became stiff and had a dull ache in it. I rubbed on a little of every kind of ointment and grease I could find. They certainly didn't do any harm but neither did they do much good. I didn't go to see a doctor because I had a sneaking notion that he would tell me not to run until the knee got well, which would probably be after April 19 or at least after I had lost the fine condition I had built up from practicing all winter.

It has been my experience all through my running career that often I get painful spots in a knee or the calf of a leg or a foot, but nothing of that kind prevents my running except a sore hip. My sore knee may have been caused by a slightly crooked spine, which in turn caused an awkward gait and undue exertion on one knee. I never found out whether this theory was scientifically justified, but it seems a logical one.

Once a sore calf was caused by the overzealous massage of a rubber after a race. This slight pain lasted for years. Now I always try to be on my guard against "rubbers" after a race. There are always some amateur and professional rubbers present after every marathon. Once at Port Chester, a rubber approached me, and more to oblige him than anything else I let him put alcohol on my legs and slap it around. He turned out to be a professional to the extent of a dollar fee, so since then I have hardened my heart against such generous offers.

Just a few nights before the B.A.A. in 1911, in my sleep I dreamt distinctly that I had won the big race. Of course I know such things are just a coincidence, but I was glad of the encouragement. One or two runners thought I might win and just one newspaper, the old Boston Journal, had an item in Bob Dunbar's Column, saying, "Watch DeMar, he might win in fast time."

Before the race, as usual, the staff of doctors examined all the contestants and advised one or two not to start. They listened quite a while at my chest and gave the verdict that this should be my last race and I should drop out of it if I got tired. They said that I had heart murmurs. I do not know whether it is possible to run a marathon in competition and not get tired, but at any rate I've never done it. At the finish one doctor expressed much surprise at how well I had run. He didn't ask whether I had become fatigued or not.

I certainly had been tired but not exhausted. I just ran with a determination that made me confident of doing the job. At 19 miles I took the lead from Festus Madden and won by a half mile in 2:21:39 3/5, taking about three minutes off Tom Longboat's record. My sore knee had stayed just the same throughout the race and was no worse after it.

For this victory I received a large bronze "chariot of victory" with a special gold medal for breaking the record. And of course there was plenty of publicity and ballyhoo, which was very stimulating and amusing for a while. I received a number of post cards and letters from presumably pretty girls, but this was not repeated after my wins in the twenties, although I was still unmarried. Perhaps my face acquired too many wrinkles with the years. A man's face looks worse than usual after he finishes a marathon, anyhow. Bill Kennedy used to object to having his picture taken when he finished, saying that his wife always remarked on how old he looked!

I accepted an invitation to a ball held by the North Dorchester A.A. under whose colors I had won. While there, an athletic official looked at my thin features with some admiration for what I had done, but more pity that I didn't have more flesh. He remarked: "You don't drink ale, do you? That is too bad, for a glass a day would build you up in no time." Later, when I heard he was very sick I wondered if it could be that he had forgotten his daily ale.

The employees of the Rand Avery Supply Company, then on Franklin Street, where I was working, gave me a stick pin with a chip diamond, but one of the executives down in the office told me that what I needed was a Turkish bath to freshen my overworked muscles. He further said that if I didn't have the price of this luxury he'd make that all right.

Generous enough, but I was getting $8.00 per week with considerable overtime! During the day the Boston American called up the shop and wanted to know if I was working. The foreman good naturedly said, "I told them you were here, but I wasn't sure whether you were doing much work." But I was working and one point of my philosophy of life has always been never to let running interfere with my daily work. On the day after a marathon I always feel as if I had been out late the night before, yet I'm sure I've always done a fair day's work.

During that summer I got up to Vermont and found the natives of South Hero supposed I had received a lot of money for my victory. With Yankee instinct they were disappointed that the only gain had been a statue and a medal.

For a great many years I was more conscientious about observing the letter as well as the spirit of the amateur code than now. In 1911 I got a number of invitations to race with good expenses. Once I was asked to run in Worcester; they were willing to pay taxi fare out and back, even if I walked. I conscientiously declined. Fifteen years later I would have taken the money and given the boy scouts a good time, and twenty-five years later I'd have taken it and fed my family, rationalizing that I had spent lots more than this wind-fell from my own pocket during the times I attended the Olympic Games. This might be described as the evolution of a conscientious amateur. At twenty-three he refuses money; at thirty-eight he accepts and uses for boys' organizations; at forty-eight he accepts and uses for his family with the mental excuse that the game owes it to him; at seventy I may accept and use the money to keep myself out of the poor house, but we shall see.

I also had an invitation, after that first race, to run in St. Louis with legitimate expenses of $50.00 and hotel bills, but I refused because of my work. Then someone wanted a race between several local runners and me, on a track. They were willing to give me almost any piece of jewelry I wanted for a prize. I kept refusing partly because everyone had advised me that I needed a rest and partly because, with my youthful idealism, I felt there was something wrong about the amateur side of that particular contest. Now I know that undoubtedly the promoters hoped to make something, but that the odds were against them, because people will pay so little to see a foot race. Anyhow, as a last resort, after several refusals to run on my part, one smooth-talking runner, long-since retired, told me that if I was afraid of getting beaten after my splendid victory I need have no fear for he would "fix" that all right. I told him there was no need to "fix" anything since I would prefer to win my share on my own merits. Only twice in twenty-seven years have I heard any such suggestion. So, on the whole, amateur running is a very fair thing.

On May 30, I ran in a 15-mile race at one of the big league parks. As I recall it there were a number of contestants and only a few paid spectators. Albert Home of Everett (often called Belly-ache Home) led for over half way, then, true to his name, he got a pain and I gained and held the lead to win in about 1:27.

For nearly two months after the big marathon that year I had a hacking cough. I don't know whether this was caused by reducing too much for the race or whether it was just a natural threat of T.B. at a susceptible age. While it didn't interfere with my work and didn't seem to slow up my running, it had me worried and was especially bad just after a race. Finally, someone said, "You can get rid of that cough easy enough; take Scott's Emulsion." I did so and that time it stopped the cough in about a week. However, I do not especially recommend this to everyone with a cough, for my experience with many cures for minor ailments is that they sometimes work the first time for some people and never again for those people and only rarely for anyone else. There are great individual differences and great differences in the same individual from month to month and year to year. These differences apply especially to athletes and their problems for getting into condition and staying there and make training a matter which cannot be standardized but requires judgment and ingenuity with a frequent shift of plans and schedules.

Early in June, I ran a 10-mile handicap race for the Dorchester Day celebration. I got third and time. Then on June 17 I ran another 10-mile handicap at Danvers. Here I won first and time. That was the first occasion I ever recall getting any "expenses" to run. The manager handed me two dollars and said, "Give Dick Piggott one." The dollar covered everything, but when I think of the way expenses came in the twenties, I realize that amateurism is only relative. For this race I received two beautiful loving cups. Someone visiting my mother in a day or two and seeing the cups, remarked that it was most unusual for anyone to win another race after they had won the marathon! That notion that a man is through, once he wins the B.A.A., persists with nothing to back it except a few isolated cases, such as the subsequent failure of Renaud, after his victory in 1909; and the failure of Miles to do anything so phenomenal as his victory in 1926, although he won the big race again in 1929.

A week after the Danvers race I won a 10-mile scratch run on the track at Canobie Lake. Tom Lilly and I sort of teamed up to pace each other from the start and go fast to prevent Cliff Home of Haverhill, then a coming runner, from making a showing by leading for a few miles, which he liked to do when his friends were present. We succeeded, which shows that I had developed to where I could do better than a 5:30 mile and kept it up for nearly five miles. The time for the whole race was under 57 minutes. The race was so late that I could only get a trolley as far as Reading and had to walk the rest of the way, getting in at 2 A.M.

I didn't have any more races for nearly two weeks, until July 4 when I ran a 10-mile scratch race in Somerville. The day was probably the hottest of any I ever ran on. It took me quite a bit over the hour to do the distance, but I had no need to hurry, for the second man, Jordan of Cambridge, a cousin of another marathoner, was about a mile back, and all the other contestants quit. As they had eight prizes and only two finishers I managed to collect two.

Some time after this I was invited to run an exhibition one-mile at an affair on the Readville track. This is a mile horse-track so I had just one lap for the exhibition. I never could do a mile very fast and this being an exhibition, 1 didn't practice especially or key myself up much. So it took me 5:45 to make the round. The announcer kindly called it 4:45. I received a cut-glass set for the appearance, but no "expenses" of any kind.

Then I had quite a rest until about the middle of August when I was invited up to Manchester, New Hampshire for a 10-mile scratch race held by the Foresters. This run was from Manchester to Goff's Falls. I got there just a few minutes before starting time and at once sensed a tenseness among the other runners. My record for the year had been seven victories and no defeats. Naturally the others were beginning to feel that it was somebody else's turn to win, so they had patched up a little plan. As soon as the race started a couple set a pace faster than 5:30 per mile which was too fast for any of us to keep up more than three miles in a 10-mile race. But they kept it up right along and I, full of pride at my year's successes, stayed with them. At five miles I felt very tired but did not dare drop the leaders lest I lose my stride and fell way back. At seven miles the ones who had planned on killing me off, for that was the plot, dropped back to give Dick Piggott or Tom Lilly a chance to come up from the rear and beat me the last three miles. Just at this point the officials hollered, "Turn in here," and behold that was the finish! I won in 39 minutes; it was seven miles instead of the ten as advertised. That is a thing we have to be on our guard against in a 10-mile race over a strange course; it may be anywhere between six and fourteen miles. As to the runners' little plot to tire me out, if they had but known that it was only seven miles they probably could have beaten me running naturally without a plot, for that was a little too short a distance for me and the only victory for the year at less than 10-miles. The immense trophy awarded for this short race is now in my mother's house in Melrose. The prize is as large as any I ever got for a marathon, and often visitors comment on the discrepancy in size between that trophy and several small cups for 20-mile races, for instance.

During the summer of this year I received a letter from Dr. Kellogg of Battle Creek, Michigan. (This is not the Kellogg of cornflake fame.) The doctor had some ideas on diet, which he said should improve my endurance. He invited me to spend a few weeks at his sanitarium and find out for myself. Since I couldn't afford to lose my wages for the sake of the doctor's experiment I declined, but expressed my interest in the matter and my willingness to eat as he would suggest for a year or so. So Dr. Kellogg wrote me a lot about calories, proteins, carbohydrates and fats and the advantages of abstaining from meat. With the cooperation of my mother I conscientiously followed the program of eating no meat (except Thanksgiving) and tried to count the proper number of calories for a year. When I went away from home or anyone visited us, it was embarrassing to have to explain about my eating habits. Many people thought me "persnickety" but I felt that my running would be more justified if I contributed something to the noble experiment in science! After eating this way for a couple of months I saw no change for better or worse. Then came the Brockton marathon. Dr. Kellogg especially advised me what to eat the morning of the race. It was: one dozen oranges, 1/4 lb. pine nuts, and one pound of high grade caramels which he sent. I found that it took nearly the whole morning to eat all this stuff. The oranges, especially, took a long time for no one was as used to eating oranges then as now. After this marathon of eating I didn't feel especially full of pep, but found I had plenty of endurance in the race. I won, taking the lead at Dutchland Farms and having a comfortable margin at the finish.

After this Dr. Kellogg was pleased and had a big piece in one of his papers about my victory with a vegetable diet. At heart I couldn't get away from the thought that I probably would have won anyhow, and that if the experiment had any scientific value it was simply to show that a person could have plenty of endurance without meat for some months. However, the idea of becoming better than the other runners by having a better diet was fascinating, so I intended to continue. I didn't plan to do any more competing as Mr. Babb of Melrose, prominent as an A.A.U. member, and others had assured me my prospects for next year's Olympic team were better without more racing. So I passed up the New England 10-mile championship held in Lynn that year. This gave me a year without defeats and ten victories, including two marathons. I felt I had accomplished the second highest ambition of a marathoner—to win the B.A.A. (The highest honor is, of course, to win the Olympic race.) And 1 was satisfied to have held the honor without defeat for the entire year.

I heard someone say: "Won the big race, did he? Well he must be the happiest boy in the world." I'm quite sure I was not, however, because, with a natural ambition to better myself, I felt that the B.B.A. was only a step, and I still longed to win an Olympic Marathon. What's more the victory did not seem to bring respect, only a kind of curiosity as to why I had done it, and the desire to give me some advice. Advice, always advice! I still had just as many problems of finance and personal adjustment as anyone, so for all these reasons, I wasn't as contented as I might have been. The year 1911 remained a year of improvement and achievement in running stunts, but 1 still had no feather in my cap for personal poise or happiness.

Chapter 4
How Does it Feel to
Run a Marathon?

"What does a fellow think about when he's running one of those long grinds?" How many times have I been asked that! Whatever I may think myself may not apply to others, but some of the general things that go through a marathoner's mind will be the same. I have asked several runners, including Jimmie Henigan, and while they differ on just what they think about, all agree to a tenseness and fear and uncertainty about something.

Jimmie, for instance, says he is always wondering whether he will finish or not. That particular fear has crossed my mind very few times; for I always feel sure that I can finish if I slow up. Another runner, not so experienced, always wondered whether he'd be running in a good position when he passed his native town less than half way through. Still another worries for fear he won't get through in time for any refreshments at the finish unless he rides. Another has to go to work for the night and is uncertain about the exertion tiring him too much. All have their fears and worries exaggerated by the tenseness of the competition.

But let's start at the beginning of a typical Boston Athletic Association (B.A.A.) marathon and describe a few phases. This will be mostly the 1936 race. Here I am just reaching Framingham, via bus. As I stroll across the street someone says, "That's him!" Another says, "Aw no, DeMar's taller." Then to settle it the first hollers, "Hi, Clarence." My feelings were mixed. Should I ignore the salutation as I often did in such cases, or turn and speak? He probably did not want my autograph and the people of Framingham have been loyal athletic friends of mine, so I smiled and said "Hey." "Hope you win," said one. "Good luck," chimed in the other.

Reaching the hotdog cart, I judged that there was no great turnover of employees there, for one recalled my having eaten with them off and on for a generation before the race, and the service they gave me was A-1. Dropping into a store I bought some oranges and prunes to chew on during the evening and the next morning. There was no escape from the people in Framingham. "How good is the Indian?" asked one clerk. "Great, if he hasn't too many handlers," I answered. "You like it hot, don't you?" asked another man. "Yes, the heat always kills off some of my rivals," I agreed. "When is the next bus to Hopkinton?" I asked. "In twenty minutes, why don't you run up?" one helped.

I walked about a quarter of a mile when someone opened the door of a car and said "Get in DeMar, I'm going right up to Hopkinton." He proudly introduced me to the other man in the auto and then as he stopped for gas asked the man at the filling station if he knew who I was. "Oh yes, I've watched him run since I wore knee pants," replied the man. In a few minutes we had covered the five miles to the Marathon Inn at the start. "Guess you will find a lot of them up there," remarked the man who had given me the ride. "Oh, that's too much of a home-coming for anyone who wants all his energy for the race," I replied, "I stop across the road with the Halleys. Here's the house, right here."

Mr. and Mrs. Halley and her sons gave me the usual welcome and said that my room was ready. She asked when I wanted breakfast and promised me the usual protection from fans and autograph-seekers the next morning. She even cautioned her sons that if they were out late to return quietly. A long night in bed with the cool Hopkinton air blowing in, and quite a bit of sleep, in spite of a certain tenseness that never foils in anticipation of the big contest, made me feel fresh and hopeful the next morning. Up by seven I arranged for my breakfast of cereal, toast, and eggs at nine, ate several oranges and went for a stroll.

Out a couple of hundred yards near the start I found one fourth-rate runner of the two hundred odd expected starters also looking things over. "Hello DeMar," he greeted me, "Don't you remember me? I lead the Bunker Hill race for three miles. I'm — from Framingham." "You must be pretty good, then," I replied, "Good luck to you." "Say," he whispered, "Do you suppose they will let me run without the dollar entry fee?" "Sure," I replied, "Of course the B.A.A. is awful hard up, but since you are here, I'll bet it will be OK, and, oh yes, tell them you'll pay them next year." "No," he answered, "I won't make them wait that long, but will mail the buck soon as I get paid by the W.P.A."

At about ten the busses arrived from Framingham with the rest of the runners, the officials and doctors. A lot of athletes and their friends had already come by private car so there were scores of those parked about. I thought I might as well get the physical exam over and also get my number, so I walked towards the inn. But I couldn't get near the house without signing autographs. And yes, there was Humbert Cirafice, as usual, with entry blanks for his twelve-mile race in Lynn next month. "We hope you can come down, Clarence," he coaxed, "Can't promise," I laughed. "Might be in Boston that weekend and need the exercise, but probably not."

Besides the "camp followers" there were others with more business, including reporters, officials and runners. I overheard, "How do you figure this race?" "Oh, I like Pawson, but I'm always expecting old man DeMar to fool them again sometime— Oh, there he is! How are you Clarence? Going to win, today?"

"Say you fellows give me a pain," I replied, "always asking a decrepit old cuss nearly fifty to win."

"Yes," agreed Bill Kennedy. "It's that way with me, too. As I left home nearly a dozen hoped I'd win, and I told each of the damn fools that there were at least twenty in the race with a better chance than I."

"We'd better not let him run," joshed a doctor as he recognized me. But after a weighing in, a pulse, heart and blood pressure test, they said that I was as good as ever, so far as they were concerned. I wandered through the runners' rooms of the inn and saw about every runner of note that I could think of. But more noticeable than the runners was the stench of rub down, with a mixture of alcohol, witch hazel, wintergreen and lesser-known substances. And what a mess for someone to clean up, with newspapers, bottles and boxes scattered everywhere. The B.A.A. gets a bargain when it pays fifty dollars for the use of the inn during the forenoon.

Few runners have gone to the slight extra expense to hire a separate dressing room in another house like myself. Even Johnny Kelly, the favorite to win, was cramped up in a corner, looking thin and determined. My unexpressed comment was that it was funny his friends hadn't thought of hiring a room in the neighborhood. Still, I observed the golden rule in this case and made no comment. What were the babel, bad smells and lack of privacy in comparison to the distraction of a free piece of advice! And in a year or two he'd probably find out for himself!

On the way back to my private house I had to pose for several fans with cameras, but I finally escaped. Even here, a fellow from Pennsylvania, who had stayed in the room next to mine with the Halleys a few marathons back, came to call. In being courteous to this man I neglected to check in at the start fifteen minutes early. With ten minutes to wait I arrived at the bullpen, to be officially recorded as on hand. George Brown was nerved up and displeased at my irregularity. However, I had a feeling that no one would accuse me of being down the road a few miles when the gun went off so took my place with the mass of contestants without officially checking in.

With five minutes to wait the newspapers wanted a picture. "All the hams are up front, get a few good ones," exclaimed one. So by request a few of us former winners were privileged to lead before the race began, and incidentally the picture would prove that I was at the start. At the crack of the gun on the stroke of twelve there was a scramble, but as usual by holding out my elbows, like a chicken about to fly, I protected myself. And, as always, I was fortunate enough not to have anyone step on my heel and pull the shoe off.

In less than half a mile I began to feel very tense and somewhat like the foreman of a print shop with a lot of work piled up, or perhaps an editor with a scoop coming in ten minutes before the presses started. All my faculties were being concentrated on the race and it was about as natural for me to do this as it would be for a dog to walk on his hind legs or a college student to do some thinking. My physical distress at having my heart, lungs and legs work at abnormal speed and the mental difficulty of keeping my body at the task was such that the one thing I dreaded was interruption or distraction of any kind. Any word or deed aimed to get my attention would be like throwing a monkey wrench into a finely geared piece of machinery. Just a personal word like "Step on it there" or "Get going, Clarence" and I felt furious. But of course the impersonal yelling and cheering was a slight encouragement.

Any exhortations which annoyed me would be exaggerated many times if they came from an intimate friend. Sometimes with the wild imaginations of the contest I think anything but loving, friendly thoughts about my special friends, just imagining them making little trivial inconsequential suggestions that we might win. I much sympathize with the runner who told me he hated to have his wife go to races. But she insisted that she didn't marry him to be put on a shelf, so he put up with her occasionally.

As I tore down on the light side of the road through Ashland how afraid I was that someone would bother me. Was the fear increased because I was running, or did I run better because I was afraid? Ask the psychologists, I don't know. But here came a distraction from the rear. The official cars were coming from the start to join the leaders. As they came along they kept making the runners move over to the left to let them get by easier. I was puzzled as to what I'd say when they told me to move over as I felt the race was for runners, not official cars, yet I've always had a feeling of gratitude to the B.A.A. for their excellent management of their marathon and hated to bawl them out even if I was tense and concentrated. My dilemma was solved by a runner just in back snapping, "Get on over there yourself." "Oh," said the official, "if that is the way you feel, okay." "Nice running, Clarence," they encouraged, as they passed on the left

Approaching Framingham, while in a group of seven or eight, a contestant kept running in front of me and slowing up. This annoyed me a little, but nothing like the insane anger caused by meddlesome fans, as I'm always sympathetic with contestants, knowing they are working as hard as I. And I knew further that it was natural to hustle while behind a man you wanted to beat and to slow up as soon as you were ahead. So three or four times I merely ran around the pest and said nothing. But pretty soon he was doing the same thing to Johnny Semple. The second or third time Johnny exploded in good Scotch brogue, "You blooming fool, what's the idea?" No waste of energy or anything else for Scotch Johnny if he could help it!

Rounding a curve approaching Framingham a press car was in my way. "Let me have the inside, will you?" I shouted. Obligingly they stopped and opened the door of their sedan. "The inside of the curve, of course," I yelled, and rushed on. Passing through Framingham close to the ropes a man reached out, slapped me on the chest, and yelled, "Hi buddy, remember Saint Amand!" A marathon is no time to reminisce!

With periods of tenseness and fear of distraction alternating with periods of comparative calm I continued, the pendulum of distress and ease swinging back and forth about a dozen times during the race. From this I can truthfully say that I got not only my second wind but also tenth and twelfth wind in most marathons. But whether I'm tense or calm it is not a time for reasoning things like mathematics. Sometimes minor problems of addition, subtraction, or division present themselves in figuring how I should run some stretch in comparison to other years, considering my present condition. Sometimes it takes several miles to get an answer I could get in a minute at my desk; but I can get it and know when it is right, too.

I find many, if not most runners, like myself are afraid of meddlesomeness and resent distraction while they are competing. One man stuck his head out from a car and yelled at Pouffe of Worcester, "I'm rooting for you." "That's right, you look like a hog," replied Pouffe. The head went back into the car quickly. Someone else hollered at a young competitor, "Are you a runner?" "No, a swimmer," the boy replied, "Do you know where the next pond is?" Funny how great the barrier is between competitor and spectator.

While I can't figure mathematics easily, nor think deeply on most subjects while running with all my might, I always feel confident that I am very much master of my fate. Keyed up I am super-quick to dodge traffic and do broken field running. I am extremely alert to grab the shortest curve in the road or to get out of a troublesome bunch of competitors by ducking around autos or sidewalks. "This one thing I'm doing," as St. Paul said; only in this case it happens to be merely running a marathon race and not preaching or practicing a better life. As I put everything I am capable of into the contest, I sometimes feel that the whole world is divided, not only as Charles Lamb said, into those who borrow and those who lend, but also into those who pay attention and accomplish things and those who distract attention and are infernal nuisances. The runners are paying attention and the rest of the world is mostly trying to distract them. The possibilities for trivial questions or conversation or advice in a marathon race are almost unlimited; but the more of these distractions there are, the harder for the runners. Sometimes, as a Sunday School teacher, I have reflected that the race does not make for love and kindly feeling and I've even thought that should I die or the end of the world come while I was in a race, my heart would not have love of anyone in it, but rather a great fear of the petty distraction of well-meaning but meddlesome fans.

There are fortunately at least three partial escapes from this feeling of fear and hate for those who bother my concentration during a race. One is a sense of humor, which is present even in tense moments. For instance, while a movie machine was grinding a few feet of film of me plodding along, Pasquale, up ahead fifty yards, turned and ran back to be in the picture. And he really expects to win the big race sometime! Then I get a laugh at the fans who call me Jimmie and call Henigan, Clarence.

Another escape from the fear and hate in my heart during a lot of the race has of late years been the wholehearted applause I receive over the last ten miles of the big marathon. People have nearly ceased being critical and give me more of an ovation when I'm eighteenth than they did twenty-five years ago when I was leading! A number of times I've felt tears of appreciation come into my eyes at such approval.

The third escape is the feeling of exhilaration that comes instantly once one has stopped running. What a lot of cheerful chatter-boxes all the runners are when the contest is over. No old woman's sewing circle ever talked more. How they re-run this and other races! A few are somewhat boastful but none offensively so. With this relaxation and good feeling from relief of tenseness and strife I have always been over-generous and too easily imposed on for several days. Then somebody over-does it and I get back to earth.

This problem of over generosity after victory has been solved in recent years by not winning. And with all the tenseness and strife of the race and the over relaxation afterwards I have never found it to dampen my desire for the next contest. After all, do most of us want life on the same calm level as a geometrical problem? Certainly we want our pleasures more varied with both mountains and valleys of emotional joy, and marathoning furnishes just that.

Chapter 5
The 1912 Olympics

Having been given good reason to expect that I would
be a member of the 1912 Olympic Marathon Team
without further competition and with the advice of athletic
officials and doctors that the more marathons one ran, the
less his chance of winning, I went contrary to my intuition
and followed their advice and laid low during the spring
of 1912. While I did plenty of practice running, yet by
doing as other people suggested in keeping out of
competition, I was beginning a year which brought
experience proving what I might already have known, that
I should be myself, and not put myself out to do as other
people said.

Sometime before the B.A.A., Lawrence Sweeney of
the Boston Globe wrote a feature article about my going
to the Olympics. During our conference he asked if I
thought anyone would ever win the B.A.A. twice again.
He continued, "You know you are a whole year older next
time." He shook his head when I replied: "I have a feeling
that if a good runner concentrated on that one race and
prepared especially for it from year to year he could win it
not only twice, but a great many times."

When the 1912 B.A.A. was held it rained, and with the incentive of a trip to Stockholm to stimulate them, the young field set a fast pace. I watched it from a press car. Sockalexis looked like a winner until after Coolidge Comer, when Mike Ryan, big, strong, and covered with grease, crashed through not only to win, but also to break my record by 21 seconds. Sockalexis was second, very close to the record, and there were four runners under Longboat's previous mark.

After a 10-mile exhibition to satisfy Mr. Babb of the Olympic committee, I was informed that I had been selected. There were twelve on that team. The other eleven were: Mike Ryan of the Irish American A.C. of New York; Andrew Sockalexis, the Indian from Old Town, Maine; Dick Piggott of Medford; Tom Lilly of Dorchester; Gallagher of Philadelphia; Forshaw, and Erxleben of St. Louis, Tewanina, an Indian from the west also running the 10,000 meters, and John Reynolds and Harry Smith, both of New York. Sidney Hatch of Chicago was also going to be on the team but had some work that he thought was more important, so they put on Gaston Strobino of Patterson, N. J., who had done well in a big 12-mile race in New York. A team of 12 made quite a group. Nowadays we have only three from each country. In an event as uncertain as the marathon it seems to me that it would be an improvement if each nation were still allowed twelve representatives, provided that each of the twelve were allowed to work out his own system of getting into condition. Based on the way we were handled in 1912, we might just as well have had only three on the team—for having the group train together is like putting all your arrows into one quiver.

As the whole Olympic team gathered in New York prior to sailing on the Finland, which had been chartered for the trip, one of the Olympic committee members gave us quite a lecture, emphasizing that we'd better do what we were told as no one was indispensable to the team and it would be very easy to send any disobedient athlete home. The impression the talk made on us was unfavorable to say the least. To me, it seemed like an insult.

Training on the boat was so arranged that each group, sprinters, middle distance men, marathoners, walkers, bicyclers, etc. all had their turn. Some sports writers think this was the best all around track team the U.S. had until 1936. Certainly there was plenty of talent, and it was a pleasure to watch them run around the ship for an hour or two yelling "track" if anyone got in the way.

During most of our practice, Mike Ryan ran at the head of the squad and set the pace. Somehow it made me think of a herd of beef critters with the leading bull ahead. Mike had made a new record and we tried to respect him for it, although he was rather dominating. For instance, he would try to trip me up if I talked and he would bawl me out if I kept quiet for not saying anything. Once as I was eating cherries at the meal table and chucking the seeds out the port hole, one by one; I missed and one bounced down and hit Mike's head, which at that time was red. Glaring at me, he yelled, "Have you no table manners?" There were many such incidents involving different members of the team and it was hard to please the "leader."

Mike Murphy of Pennsylvania was head coach and Johnny Hayes, the winner of the marathon at the previous Olympics at London, was the special trainer of the marathon team. Murphy had no objections to my continuing the diet experiment. There was plenty to eat without meat, so I got along very well. With regard to the food on the boat, the weight throwers, of course, ate more than the other people. There was a tendency on the part of Mike Murphy to watch and see that no one ate too much jam or other sweets. Like any group, whether they have the best or the worst food, these athletes did some complaining at times. Murphy's comment was, "The less they have to eat at home, the more they kick about the food when they're away." One other remark of his about the food has always stayed with me. In Stockholm the beer wagon brought the bottles around each morning, just as they do milk in this country. That gave those who weren't abstainers, like myself, plenty to drink. One day Coach Murphy announced: "Some of you fellows are dissipating. You are drinking both milk and beer; now cut it out, drink all the milk or all the beer you want, but not both!"

Finally, we stopped at Antwerp to get in some practice and to break up the length of the trip. One of the local papers published an account about "a whole boatload of American millionaires being in town." (Some of us had as much as $50.) Everywhere we went there were kids begging *d'argent* and girls looking for handsome athletes. After we had left and were up in the Baltic Sea I overheard one of the officials say, "A great team if they are but in condition." And the other replied, "Yes, I hope we don't strike another place like Antwerp."

While at the Belgium city we practiced each day in a hay field nearby. Murphy and Hayes watched us run about twenty miles each time. We didn't race, but neither did we loaf. I didn't feel as carefree and confident as I would with a goal towards which I could aim each day without critical eyes on me. Here I felt I had to make good each day whether I were racing or not. Alone I'd have run much slower part of the time.

So, I was rather tired as we steamed down the Scheldt River to continue our journey. Once in the narrow river the big boat rammed the bank. Dick Piggott exclaimed, "Gosh I never knew the English Channel was so narrow as this, I thought it was much wider." But I'll bet they teach geography much better than that in Medford now.

When I arrived at Stockholm the first night I felt I should stretch my legs ashore and so made for the gang plank. Mat Halpin of New York, the manager of the team, met me and asked where I was going, then snapped, "I should say not, you are staying right on board." Possibly after Antwerp the officers felt they should "do Stockholm first." In that case a general notice posted would have prevented such humiliation to keyed-up athletes. One of my maxims has always been: "If you want men to be champions, then treat them like champions, not puppets."

Because the race was only a couple of weeks away, we had to train intensively. As at Antwerp I strained every nerve to please the coaches each day instead of using my own foresight as when unwatched.

One official said that either Ryan, DeMar, or Sockalexis must win this race for us. So we all got plenty of attention and they neglected poor Strobino who had been put in at the last day as a filler. In view of the way the race came out, this is significant to me. Not only did they watch, but Hayes, like the young man in Vermont who tried to urge me to run on my toes and did his urging while I was tense and in motion, frequently made nagging suggestions about stride and position of the body as we ran. I've always stated that when I get through with amateur running at least I'll get out of the way and stay there and not hamper the future champions by trying to tell them something which they don't want me to.

But don't think the "land of the free" was the only one having tyranny in the coaching staff. One day I asked the Canadian group: "Do the blooming coaches bother you fellows?" Joe Forsythe from Winnepeg answered quickly, "If my father ever spoke to me the way the coaches do, he'd be short a good farm-hand right away!" I have never checked on many other nations, but wouldn't it be a paradox if we found that in coaching at the Olympic Games "the democracies were tyrannical and the tyrannies democratic?"

Eventually, a week or so before the race, with the nervous strain of trying to make good every day instead of once a fortnight, I went stale—that is, I got so tired that I couldn't freshen up in a day, or two. I was very lame and I had ruptured a blood vessel from the strain of too much practice. So with all this trouble I wasn't much of a runner when the race came.

Before I describe the race I might say that the marathoners and Jim Thorpe, the great all-around athlete, were stationed in fine quarters a few miles out at Stocksund. Mike Murphy found time to be with us frequently. During one of his pep talks he said: "And Smith, (one of us) you keep away from these Swedish girls, I don't want to see you talking to them again."

This Smith (it's "His Honor, Harry Smith" now) was not quite a champion marathoner in those days. But he did do some scouting around to watch the runners from other countries. Finally he gave this verbal report. "I've watched marathoners from Canada, England, India, South Africa, France and Japan, and after looking them all over I've reached the conclusion that they are all a bunch of nuts—that is all except us."

The morning of the race some of the Catholic boys including Mike Ryan of our team and Jimmie Duffy of the Canadians, went to mass. Having a strong urge for religious things, I went with them.

This marathon was the only one where at the start they plotted and drew for each position, having a sort of military squad instead of a huddle. The day was very hot and after the half-way mark (we ran out and back over the same route) the pace was slower. A Portuguese runner got sunstroke and died the next day. This is the only time I was ever in a race that resulted in a fatality.

Soon after the halfway point Mike Ryan quit the race. I believe one other American also quit, and the rest of us finished somehow. I was hopelessly outclassed and had to walk about a mile. This and the Halifax, Nova Scotia, marathon in 1927, are the only two times in my life that I have ever broken my running stride in sixty-five marathons. MacArthur of South Africa finally won, with a teammate second and the ignored Gaston Strobino third, putting the American flag up at least. As a large team we made a good showing, although that was not so difficult in those days when other nations didn't have the athletes that they do today. We had seven men in the first twelve where I finished.

I was much the lamest after that race of any before or since and had to carry a cane for a week, as did others.

That was the result of forcing myself through the race when not in condition.

While at Stockholm, we saw some great races, including the mile in which our men: Jones, Tabor Sheppard, Hedlund, and Kiviat (acknowledged the best in the world) were so anxious to beat each other that they neglected the rest of the field and Jackson, an Englishman, made a last half-lap dash to win. We also saw the close 5000 meter race between Kohlemainen of Finland and Bouin of France with the Finn winning by a yard.

We all appreciated the great showing of the Finns. They were a kind of down-trodden part of Russia then, although they had a separate flag. They had not yet become good enough for us to be jealous. As we got all three places in the 100-meter dash, Finland won first, second and third in the javelin throw. The result was three Finnish flags all alone on the posts of honor. So our cheerleader called for cheers for Finland, and the 1912 group could cheer!

Immediately, the Olympic committee gave us a call, saying to cheer only for ourselves, as Russia might be offended if we cheered for Finland!

After the games King Gustaf sent over saying that he'd like to meet the great American athlete Jim Thorpe. We all knew how matter of fact he took the great honors, which he won. Thorpe meditated a moment, yawned, stretched, and said, "I guess I won't go!" and so the king has not yet met Thorpe!

A few of us stayed to visit England. The managers gave us an order for first class passage to Boston or New York. A couple of us managed to swap these orders for second-class tickets and over forty dollars. That increased the spending money a great deal. Afterwards, however, the clerk found a small clause on the order that forbade such an exchange. But the best he could do was to refrain from giving it to the rest for neither of us had the forty dollars intact the next day. Harry Smith and I roomed together for a very low rate. We also found eating places where we could get meals for about a nickel each. There were lots of bums hanging around who would beg for what was left. We'd usually give the first one who asked the whole dish and then buy another for ourselves. In 1912 these bums were the most conspicuous things in London, just as soldiers were the most noticeable things on the continent. In less than two years, the soldiers, and the bums made into soldiers, were to be put to work murdering each other.

The English woman who kept the boarding house where Smith and I stayed was very nice indeed. She took a motherly interest in us and would sit up nights until we both got in, fearing that we'd get lost in the big city. I'm sure her concern was genuine, as we'd paid her in advance.

A small party including George Brown, the official, Al Gutterson, the broad jumper, Oscar Hedlund, the miler, and myself came from Liverpool to Boston on the Canadian, which later sunk in the World War.

The 1912 team was a great one and as a whole they did very well indeed. If many of us failed to be at our best, we did not fail in vain if we knew the reason why and did not let it happen again. That is what I had impressed on me in 1912 and it helped me the next time I went in 1924.

Chapter 6
I Take a Rest....

After returning from Stockholm and getting back into my old habits of self-supervised training, I finished the year by running some pretty good races. For instance, I recall winning a 10-mile on a track one evening in Haverhill, Mass., in under fifty-seven minutes. I remember, also, receiving a letter from Mr. William Jepson, who taught a young men's Bible class in Melrose, of which I was a member, who spoke highly of this race. After a year of seeming failure it was encouraging to do some little thing that people thought had merit.

A little later I had a 20-mile race from Old Town to Bangor, with the last mile around a track. At that time I was quite busy in the printing plant of the Rand Avery Company and was working nights. Perhaps before I go on with the story of this race I had better explain that after one year on the vegetable diet under Dr. Kellogg's advice, I wrote him immediately after the Olympic marathon that I was discontinuing the experiment. While my failure at Stockholm had been in no way due to the diet, I could not see that the self-denial did one iota of good and it was a tremendous bother.

So now I ate as circumstances permitted. As I was working the night before this 20-mile race I merely sent out and got a cheese sandwich and a piece of apple pie and ate them with my inky fingers, while working. Yet taking the sleeper at the North Station at 10 P.M., I ran a good race the next day beating the field, including Sockalexis who had been fourth at Stockholm. So much for being fussy about what you eat for any particular race!

When the Brockton Fair marathon came around I didn't feel that I should waste a day's pay to run, so in the fall of 1912 began a rest from marathoning which was to last about five years. There were really other reasons. The frequent warnings of the doctors and fans of the danger to one's heart if he kept up running had left their impression. Second, as before indicated, I took my religion somewhat seriously. As a member of the Baptist church I had a suspicion that the whole game of running was a selfish vain-glorious search for praise and honor. Ministers had even preached sermons on my success, and churchmen shook hands cordially and asked about my last run. Yet I somehow felt that running for selfish victory was not the best thing I could do. I'm wondering if the Puritans may not have felt as I did, and at the present time I know that when the Olympic Games came to Amsterdam, Holland, in 1928, some of the Protestant church leaders opposed it as a "carnival of the flesh" and advised their constituents to stay away. Incidentally, their advice aroused the curiosity of people so much that the attendance at the games was the greatest of any to that date!

And the final reason for my taking a rest from the marathon game was that I didn't have time to do it properly. I had my work as a compositor, which was a reasonably hard job. Then I was taking University Extension courses at Harvard and Boston University and the attendance at classes and study took a lot of my evenings for intensive training when I should have been sleeping. So for medical, religious and business reasons I ran no marathon (25 miles or more) after Stockholm until we got into the World War. But while I did no marathons I certainly did some running incidental to my other activities. Therefore, I cannot answer the question, "What would happen if you quit running altogether?" Most fans think I'm as tied up with running as a smoker is with his weed, or a drinker with his liquor, and that for me to quit would cause nervous and physical disaster. Unless I lose a leg, become bedridden, or go to jail I never intend to find out whether this is right.

While I no longer ran all of the way home from Boston I usually ran both ways from the North Station to 117 Franklin Street where I worked. That was nearly a mile and I could do it under six minutes through traffic with my clothes on. Then occasionally I took in a little 5 or 10 mile race. There were two or three such in 1913. But I hadn't practiced much and had been studying nights so the other runners and people watching were sure I was all done winning.

In 1914 I did a few more runs. I recall taking part in some running events at the Melrose celebration on July 4. These were not sanctioned by the N.E.A.A.U. and as the papers next day gave a summary of my getting a second, my brother Robert a third and by some mistake "Charles" DeMar a fourth in the same event, the family received three letters from Mr. Facey saying that Clarence, Robert, and Charles DeMar had been suspended indefinitely by the A.A.U. And there never was any Charles DeMar until July 20, 1934, when we so named our third baby! So, owning to some reporter's slip our poor baby was fired out of the A.A.U. nineteen years before he was born!

In the fall of 1914 I began to teach a Sunday School class of seven or eight thirteen-year-old boys. I soon found that while my religion might seem to point to the folly of athletic achievement, my former athletic successes of which they had heard gave me a place in the hearts of the boys, which was a great asset in teaching. They'd come up to my house, admire my prizes and make remarks about what a great runner I had been some years ago when I was younger! I had reached the age of twenty-six, which many people then thought past a racer's prime.

That attitude repeatedly expressed had finally left an impression on me, although I doubted if it were so.

About this time I got reinstated from the suspension of the previous July 4 and took in a 5-mile race at Lowell on Oct 12. This race was at the Old Bunting Club. In searching for the dressing room I entered three different barrooms in succession. I guess the members of that club were not all athletes. This race was won by Kyronen, then the national 5-mile champion, with Weeks, the New England Champion second and I got third beating Jimmie Henigan, which shows that notwithstanding my "taking a rest," I was not in bad shape.

The B.A.A. throughout 1913, '14, and '15 was won in only fair or slow time. Ryan's record was never threatened. All the time, I had a feeling that if I curtailed my extra activities, aside from earning a living I could either win or come very near it. But I wasn't particularly anxious to do so, since with all glamour of 1911 there had been a shallowness and insincerity about much of the honor which came my way. Nevertheless, I sort of had the feeling that I could win again if I ever got around to it.

In the beginning of 1915 we called a new minister to our church in Melrose. He was the Rev. P. H. MacDowell. His strong evangelical attitude made a great stir and aroused much enthusiasm. Because of his leadership we added many new members. I still have a pleasant memory of the emotional activity,which came from church services at that time and the efforts to influence others to join. As a leader, Dr. MacDowell was almost divine in my eyes until he began to preach in favor of the World War. I couldn't see him as anything above a material opportunist in that. But at this time, 1915, when he was on such a high plane in my estimation, his friendly attitude to whatever running I had done or intended to do had its influence in keeping me from forgetting it.

I was quite busy with several University Extension courses preparing to receive my A.A degree (Associate in Arts) from Harvard in June, and also trying to get good lessons ready for my class each Sunday. I also attended most church services regularly. We even had an extra week of special services before Easter. I remember cutting a sociology class in Boston to call for several boys from my Sunday School group and take them to church to receive the opportunity and urge to "hit the trail." Several of them did and I was thrilled with joy. Yet, as the years have gone by and I see so little, if any, difference between those who took this step and those who did not, I have come to regard the whole thing as something of a vain show of physical motion for what may or may not be taking place in the heart.

After all the emotional and educational activity, I felt a desire for some physical exercise and so, with no special training other than running to and from the train, I entered a 10-mile race of St. Mary's Association in Cambridge. The run was held in a big snowstorm through the streets and around Fresh Pond. We went under the Washington Elm, not yet destroyed then. I combined historical sightseeing and athletics and looked at the tree as I passed. That was the only time I ever saw it. I finished the race somewhere in the rut. After the race Lawrence Sweeney of the Globe told me he had watched my running around the pond and that there was some running left in me yet!

On April 19 of these years (the date of annual B.A.A. classic) I usually did not bother to do more than glance at the paper to see who was entered and who won. The only year I watched the marathon between 1912 and 1917 was in 1915 when I stepped over to Exeter Street for fifteen minutes from the Public Library, where I was studying, and watched Fabre win and Cliff Home get second. But earlier in the day I had done some racing myself. I took in the 10-mile handicap race always held in Jamaica Plain. I finished ninth and received a medal. My time was under 54 minutes and although the course was probably short, I ran as fast a nine and one-half mile as ever in my life.

In June, I took two or three hours off from work in the print shop, hired a cap and gown and went over to

Harvard to receive my degree. The hundreds of learned and pseudo-learned men in hobgoblin gowns were all strangers to me, except Charlie Brickley, the great football player. He had been a member of the 1912 Olympic team for the hop-step-and-jump and so we were acquainted. He was now one of the marshals and a man of considerable distinction. He recognized me at once, took my presence in a matter-of-fact way, and found me a place in the line. Afterwards Brickley went up and down calling for those with honors to step out and go to the head of the procession. From the chuckles at the suggestion of honors I suspected that many of the men were lucky to be there.

The exercises in Sanderson Theatre were dignified and impressive, although the Latin speeches were "Greek" to me and probably to most of the audience. I was proud to have my mother attend. As President Lowell awarded the degrees it would be announced for those about to receive them to "draw near." With hundreds for one degree, only the honor men could go to the platform. But my degree, the A.A., was new then and I was the only one present to receive it so I went up all alone. As President Lowell handed it to me he said that it was in all respects the equivalent of the A.B.

Immediately after the exercises were over I had to hurry back to work, for we were very busy. One of the compositors even asked why I had taken time off. Although it was none of his business I showed him the rolled degree. He saw what it was all about, even if it was in Latin, was much surprised and said, "Don't you suppose the boss will give you another dollar a week on that?"

Soon after this graduation I became scoutmaster of Troop 5, Melrose, which met in the Baptist Church. For years I held meetings, roughhouse, hikes and had a constant come-and-go of boys. They made some progress in the requirements—probably as much as could be expected from the more or less incompetent organization and ability of the whole personnel at that time. That first troop excelled in hiking. We went Saturday afternoons and frequently stayed all night. If our organization and facilities for testing were crude at that time, our camping was even more so. While I knew enough to watch the water and sanitary conditions, we had no tents and so slept, or at least lay, on the ground all night. In case of rain we huddled around the fire and ate bacon or used our blankets for makeshift tents. The next morning a group of "half-drowned rats" would wander home to sleep all day.

I did this frequently during the proper seasons for many years and have always felt that while it was a hardship for the particular night, in the long run it made for endurance. To sleep out with a group of boys one needs to stay two nights in succession. The first night the boys, be they good or bad, disciplined or rough necks, are very restless, but are ready to sleep the second night.

Not only did we do a lot of hiking, but my troop very soon got the reputation of being one that played lots of games. The favorite game, not only with this group, but with another group after the war, has always proved to be that running game which is called either Prisoner's Base or Capture the Flag. Rules and conditions vary with circumstances. I find the rules are quickly made by common consent and I'd hate to try to play the game out of a rulebook. Sometimes we have played it in a room 30 by 40 feet or larger, sometimes out on the lawn and now and then up in the woods with small bounds or miles of territory and all day time limit. But I have yet to become the leader of a group of boys who don't prefer that game to all others. Possibly my being a runner has a lot to do with my boys always preferring a running game.

July 4, 1915 I ran the Melrose 5-mile again. The race must have been sanctioned this year or else the rule had been passed allowing unsanctioned local races. Anyhow, I won it and received a silver trophy without hearing anything from the A.A.U. I put this cup up as a prize for progress, activity and conduct in my scout troop. That was the beginning of many cups and watches I have used to motivate my boys' work. As I get older and study the matter, I am inclined to agree that the best leaders who understand their programs can get the best work without trophies for prizes.

The troop took on aspects of permanency and interest as soon as they saw the prize for the year. We enrolled some youngsters of twelve or thirteen who became intensely interested in some aspects of the program. My time and interest was so absorbed in scouting that I hardly thought of running. But about this time there was an article about the Henigan brothers and DeMar brothers and raising the question as to which could make the better team showing. Jimmie's brother Tom was doing a bit like my brother Bob so the piece made a good story. However, I'm sure the team honors belong to the Henigans, for Jimmie had by this time far outclassed me at ten miles and my brother Bob only ran once in awhile for the fun of it.

I spent April 19, 1916 in the woods with my scouts. We played Capture the Flag for most of the day. At first we tried varying the game by making it "Capture Villa" with one side raiding into Mexico and the other into U. S. But all my young patriots wanted to be Villa and raise the dickens with the United States, so we dropped the idea. My wife tells me they experience the same difficulty when Sunday Schools dramatize, "The Good Samaritan." All the boys want to be the robbers who beat up the man going down to Jericho!

That summer the troop and I went camping for a week in Ballardvale, Massachusetts, on the Shawsheen River. It was an informal camp and everyone had lots of fun. Fortunately there were no serious accidents, although we had several close calls. Three boys had to be fished out of the river.

Wishing to make the most of my week's vacation, I entered a 12-mile race that Saturday from the State House to the Scotch picnic. I practiced for over an hour Monday, Tuesday and Wednesday and in those days thought that enough for a minor race. As I was practicing through the roads of Wilmington the farmers in the hayfields would stop and gaze in wonder. One yelled, "Hey, if you want some exercise come over and work. Do something sensible."

I got second in the race and returned to sleep on the ground with the scouts Saturday night. We didn't go home until late Sunday afternoon and had amusing incidents. During the forenoon one of the inmates of the Tewksbury home for the feeble-minded came near our camp, dug a "well" high up on the sandy bank and then asked for a pail to carry water to fill it. After he had worked for some time I remarked that the fellow seemed right at home with Troop 5.

Then we had a live wire named Harry Henderson. Most of Sunday he had a hilarious time climbing trees and teasing other scouts, but when he spied his father and mother paddling up the stream, he suggested that we have the outdoor Sunday scout service. As we sat under a tree and sang, talked about the Scout laws, and had prayer with our visitors, Harry had an angelic attitude quite in contrast to his usual behavior.

But that hard week, with the race followed by another night on the ground, and my work at the shop, proved too much for me. I had to spend Tuesday and Wednesday of the next week in bed.

By this time my period of "rest" from marathoning was nearing an end. The war clouds were getting closer. It was becoming certain that our country would join the rest of the mad world. I disliked the whole business of war, but what could I do about it? If I dissented from the mad majority and went to jail my mother would miss what I did to help the family. So I decided to string along with the patriots. But if I went to war I might get killed. Why not have a little fun at marathoning first?

Chapter 7
War-Time Running

All through the spring of 1917 I prepared for the B.A.A. for the first time in six years. Naturally cautious, I only ran about three times a week, instead of my previous six. April 19th was a fairly hot day. My brother Bob rode the bicycle with me and we were pretty well back at Wellesley about seven minutes, but then began to close in. Finally, on the home stretch from Coolidge Corner I passed the great Hannes Kohlemainen, who was to win the Olympic Marathon at Antwerp in 1920. But old Sidney Hatch who had been warned that each marathon would take ten years off his life and who ran over sixty, thus greatly diminishing his chances of breaking Methuselah's record for longevity, passed me, so that at the finish it was Kennedy, first; Hatch, second; DeMar, third; and Kohlemainen, fourth. My time was about what I'd expect anyone to win in now, with the course two miles longer. It was a little over two hours and a half, but not bad for those days.

My scouts were rather pleased with my showing in the big race, although one of the best, Gerald Chandler, said, "I don't see what you let Hatch pass you for." The answer might enlighten any partisan fan who wants to know why anyone lets someone pass him in any race. "Because he was better and I couldn't help it."

The scouts and I made a war garden that summer in a vacant lot on the East Side of Melrose. That was one way the scouts did their patriotic duty during the World War.

We laughed whenever we'd dig and hit a rock, thinking of the line in "America," "I love thy rocks...." Our homes had more fresh vegetables and we all got a lot of exercise.

I used to get up at four o'clock many mornings and run the mile up to our garden, work over two hours and run back, take a splash and breakfast, then run to the train and afterwards from the train to work. Sometimes in addition I took a practice run around Spot Pond. My condition for running improved. I won the Melrose 5-mile July fourth and later got first and time at the Scotch picnic 12-mile. I will just say for the benefit of those who might be curious about it, that I have never experienced discomfort or harm from taking a run of from one to fifteen miles on the way to work immediately after a light breakfast. But then my pace is only about eight miles per hour in such runs.

When the Brockton Fair marathon came in the fall I sacrificed a day's pay and won, breaking the record. That race was run in the rain, but I had not yet reached the age when cold, wet weather slowed me up. Up to a certain point, which probably varies with individuals, rain refreshes for racing, then it makes one loggy and semi-rheumatic.

The Brockton marathon ended my competitive running until I got in the army. That fall I continued to meet and go camping with the scouts. Once, during an infantile paralysis epidemic when the schools were closed, the boys went up to Mount Hood for three days. We had been advised that the open air made it all right for a group to be together. I happened to be working late then, but as I wanted to keep in touch with scouts I ran up from the train without going home. I bought the thickest paper I could find, the Transcript, and with that for a blanket slept in the open with my clothes on. After over two years of scouting I had become so used to sleeping out that I was able to get plenty of rest that way for the long day and evening's work ahead. But it was a strenuous life and 1 had to be in good condition to enjoy it. The boys were quiet each night by the time I arrived, and that helped some.

During the recreation period that fall the boys often played a makeshift football game indoors, for with war in the air they required something strenuous. Tag football had not been invented. After the heap had piled up small boys would often mischievously jump on top. Once seeing this, I remarked to Cliff Cutting, too large to play; "That's what I think I'll do in the World War, I'll wait until they get all piled up over in Europe, then I'll go over and jump on top." That proved to be a good guess, for my military career was to be just that.

While the navy had rejected me because my printer's eyes were not far-sighted enough, the draft swept me in after a little extra examination because of a slight "runner's heart." After April 19, 1918, had passed with a relay race of service men over the course instead of the marathon, late in May I was given charge of about twenty local recruits who entrained for Camp Upton, Long Island.

In my military training at Upton and Devens and during the trip to England and then to the middle of France I had no time for running. I had all I could do to keep my gun cleaned and equipment in order for inspection without even learning how to shoot, let alone run. In feet I almost forgot about running, except once when we marched from Romsey, England to Southampton, some twenty-five miles, with packs. I found that out of a company of two hundred and fifty men only one or two had to quit. At that time I couldn't help thinking that had I been in a marathon and exerted myself as much as I did on the march I would have left at least two hundred and forty-five of the two hundred and fifty men behind. But keeping your place and pace while marching, and going as you please in competition make two very different conditions. In one you have to do as the rest do. In the other you can ease up when a wave of fatigue strikes you and go very fast when you feel like it.

Two days before Lafayette Day, Sept. 14, at St Amand, France, an announcement was made that there was to be a 3-mile race for soldiers in that area. For practice I ran three miles the night before the race. There were quite a number of starters and I had read somewhere that the army training was such that athletes and non-athletes became of equal ability in competition. This proved to be patriotic propaganda like the yam about American dyes being already as good as German; for although we athletes were not primed by preparation, and the race was in army togs, including heavy shoes, yet Fred Faller, the great 10-miler, quickly took the lead and I trailed him with the rest far in the rear. We finished in an old Roman amphitheatre where there had been gladiatorial contests two thousand years ago. This association added to the thrill of the race. Fred received ten of fifteen francs for his prize. He told me afterwards that I should have received five francs for second, but as I never got it my amateur standing was still unimpaired.

Soon after this I carelessly let a tailboard on a truck slip and gouge my leg. It was an ugly gash, but I hated to disrupt the work to speak of it. However, I did and the sergeant stopped the labor and had the truck rush me to the hospital. "Ain't you the runner?" he asked, "Well, we want you to get that leg fixed. You'll need it after the war to win some more." He proved a better prophet than most people would have drought.

One day at the hospital where I had some stitches taken in the gash, the nurse tried to redress it with a soiled bandage right on the open wound. She insisted that there were no clean bandages in the place. I said, "Leave it bare, then. I've nothing to do but shoo the flies off." A couple of hours later she came in smiling with a clean one. There was a saying in the army, "It's a great life if you don't weaken."

I argued my way out of the hospital before they wanted me to, because it was filling with the victims of a then new disease called the Spanish flu and I was afraid I'd catch it. Then, still having in mind that I was a runner who might need his leg badly, the authorities marked me "quarters" instead of "duty" for a long time, to be sure the leg was thoroughly healed. When anyone was "quarters" he was supposed to sweep the floor and stay in the barracks all the time. I always swept the floor, then went on long walks through the French woods searching among other things for a glimpse of one of the wild boars which I had seen hanging in the meat market. Had I been missed I would have landed in the pen, but this was my lucky war!

After the armistice I read in the Stars and Stripes about a race to be held in Paris on Christmas day, and so began to practice in preparation. I made application for leave to go, but such things had to go through "channels" to many officers before they reached the head of the area. Someone threw the application in the ash can. A few of us used to hire bicycles from the French and go on long rides. If stopped by a military police for not having a pass, a little humble bewilderment served to get us by, for the war was over.

Early in February I was transferred to the Army of Occupation. Our small party was stationed in a long barracks with a lot of new and old arrivals. The second day the sergeant called out, "Anyone belonging to 334th Company who wants passes can come and get them." I remarked to our group, "That company that is getting passes, I don't know just what they do, but I belong today." Sure enough, the "Sarg" never looked up as he handed over the paper. Several others of our bunch, including "Duke" Wellington of Fitchburg, Mass., got passes the same way. Then a clerk noted the mistake and checked on each man as he came, but made no effort to find where the extra passes had gone.

The first thing "Duke" and I noticed downtown in Coblenz were a lot of German children going to church with Bibles under their arms. You must understand that the children of these "atrocious Huns" we had been fighting or waiting for an opportunity to fight, had not the Koran, nor any book of Viking mythology, but the Bible with the same chapters in it about "peace on earth," that we have all read. In the church we found the pipe organ looked like the front jaw of an old person with most of his teeth gone. Over half the pipes had been melted for bullets during the emergency! Afterwards "Duke" and I visited castles, saw the beds Queen Victoria and others had slept in during visits with their German relatives, and then had an excellent feed at one of the Welfare Cantonments. Arriving at barracks for taps, no one had missed us!

One day during a conversation with a young fellow from Georgia, I lost his respect by mentioning to him that I had run twenty-five miles. He said he knew very well no one could run anywhere nearly that far and I didn't need to try to impose on him with such a yam just because he came from the mountains of Georgia. It was several days before he treated me naturally again.

Soon they began to get up educational and athletic activities to amuse the army, restless to go home. For a while I studied French and economics and stayed until the courses were completed, unlike the majority. A course would open with fifty enrolled and in about a week have fifteen left. We went to school evenings in the German School buildings, which had frosted glass in the lower window panes to prevent looking out. The rooms all had a crucifix in front and a picture of Kaiser Wilhelm in the rear. At that time all the cause of the war had been delegated to the Kaiser in person, hence naturally some soldiers in wrath tore down his picture. The "teacher" called the class down for this childish destruction, explaining that this was occupied, not conquered, territory and that the United States would have to settle for the damage.

60

After some weeks in "school" at Coblenz I made application to attend the University of Paris but the commanding officer said, "No, we have more work than our men can do now." I could have done all the work I was doing in a month in one day had I hustled. But knowing better than to argue and still wishing to see Paris after being foiled the previous Christmas as a runner and this spring as a student, and not caring to go A.W.O.L., I again turned to athletics.

I got the only pair of running shoes the supply office had and hunted up a German cobbler to stretch them. He amazed me by refusing a cent of pay. He had a cordial neighborly way with him that was good to see in that "enemy" territory.

One day a group of us were sent to Luxemburg for a track meet. There were no runs longer than the mile, but they let us distance men go and run on condition that we stay in back of the regular milers! Just a bright army regulation, but we had no trouble obeying.

Finally, I got leave to go to Paris for contests preliminary to the Interallied Games. Military discipline was practically gone so far as the athletes were concerned. So, always awkward at rolling a pack, I merely threw a few personal belongings into a blanket, tied it loosely, as I would on a Boy Scout hike, and took a train for Paris. As I was getting off I met Al Upham, who had been my partner years before in a relay race. "Gosh," he exclaimed, "You roll your pack the way they did in the Spanish War, don't you?"

I don't recall all the races I ran while on this trip, but outstanding was the sixty-mile relay from Chateau Thierry to Paris on May 30, 1919. Each team had twenty men and there were ten teams. I ran from a place called Meaux, which had been the limit of the German rush on Paris, to a point three miles in. I moved our team representing the Army of Occupation up from fourth to third, which is the place we retained at the finish.

A group of us were practicing one day and, in trying to cross the Seine to a section where Algerian troops were stationed, we were stopped by military police. We made believe we didn't understand English, but we couldn't fool him. He said he could tell Americans with or without clothes. So we ran up a way and crossed on another bridge and came down through the forbidden area, where at nighttime American soldiers had been killed in drunken brawls and their bodies thrown into the river. On our way back across the forbidden bridge we again encountered the M.P. This time he was perplexed. His orders did not cover Americans returning.

Soon I made a quick trip back to Coblenz to get my equipment and a transfer to Paris for the Interallied Games. In the trials for 10-milers I finished fourth. Only three were to run in the final race with the allies, but the fourth man was awarded a uniformed running suit as the first sub. Faller and Kennedy and one other were ahead of me. Later, other athletes from the army in the United States who hadn't been privileged to go abroad during the war, came over. That strengthened our team a good deal.

Being only a sub, of course I could not compete in the games, but was privileged to march in the opening parade of athletes. It seemed very light stepping, indeed, to walk in a running suit, after having marched with full equipment. The games, on the whole, were just a "set-up" for the United States, although we didn't win the 10-mile. Before the competition began it was interesting to go past the tents of our allied athletes and note their manners. The Czecho-Slovakians, in particular, interested me, for they had been with our enemies until just before the close of the war. They seemed interested in baseball, but will never rival the Japanese in learning it. Usually the Czechs would clap their hands shut to catch a throw, at about the same time it hit them in the stomach!

One of the novel features of these games was a camel race on the track. But the camels couldn't seem to get the idea and frequently turned and went in the reverse direction. While at Paris this time I was surprised to meet again Joe Forsythe, the Canadian marathoner, who hadn't liked the coaches any better in 1912 than I. Joe was throwing the discus this time. He said he had found marathoning too much work, and the discus much easier. But then Joe is a big fellow.

The athletes were privileged to travel to the points of interest on the battlefront. We had to be very careful not to pick up live bombs of any kind. The war had of course wrecked whole sections of France, but five years later at the Olympic Games I was surprised to find how much the damage had been repaired.

Chapter 8
I Take Another Rest

Many of us had been worried about getting a job when we returned from the war, but our difficulties were to be delayed ten years. My shop was glad to have me back, and wages were on the way up all the time. There was also frequent opportunity to work nights with time-and-a-half.

On April 19, 1920, without thought of marathoning, I took time to go canoeing on the Shawsheen with the scouts. Most of the pre-war boys had out-grown scouting, but there were a lot of new ones joining, and I usually had the full quota of thirty-two boys. One boy from a poor section of the city joined; soon many of his friends from that locality came also. Socially they were tough and even unfair at times. But they added a spirit of competition and pep and a loyalty to my troop, which I have never seen before or since. This much more than compensated for their crowding out one or two desirable members.

In holding this bunch to activities that would interest them it was necessary to have more of a boys' club than a scout troop. The program they liked best was a meet with another troop. So we arranged competitions in scout requirements, and games with other troops of Melrose, Malden and Medford for the next few years. We even sold tickets to raise money for camping, but this was a sort of graft, for not one person in ten who bought tickets came. In the competition we always arranged a relay race across the hall and back, besides relays for knot-tying and first aid. During the hours of practice we put in for these contests, I usually ran with the boys, and so didn't forget about the game, even if it was only a 25-yard dash against a fourteen-year-old boy. We often had groups together night after night in order to be in the best shape for a coming meet.

These boys, also, were particularly keen on the game "Capture the Flag." Whether it was played indoors, out on the church lawn, or up in the woods, I always played with them, although the 16-year-olds were too fast for me on a sprint. So, with running to the train, I did quite a lot of practice in 1920, even though that was the only year from 1909 to date in which I did not take in a regular race.

I might add that while these Boy Scout meets held the troop together and kept them enthusiastic, yet from a sporting standpoint they were very unsatisfactory, for how can a bugling contest, a boxing the compass race, or a first-aid exhibition for neatness be fairly judged? We had more fights and near-fights in one meet than all the nations in an Olympiad! Yet it did keep the boys interested, and we raised money for camping.

In the fall of 1920 when the Typographical Union of which I have been a member for over twenty years called a strike at the Rand Avery Supply Company for a forty-eight instead of a fifty hour week, I went out with them on general principles, although personally I was very well satisfied where I was with interesting work and good pay. It was a case of putting principles above personal choice.

For the next three months until I landed a steady situation in Medford, I got plenty of exercise hunting up jobs. How successful I was is shown by the fact that I found ten temporary positions and lost only about ten days' pay in the three months.

One odd-job I got outside had a slave-driver for a foreman. He had a nasty disposition and the average stay of his compositors then was about two weeks. I lasted three. This foreman was much laughed about by printers around Boston. One told me that after suffering this man's scolding for a week he quit. In the course of his journeying among a few of the three thousand shops of Boston, he finally came to work with a proofreader who gave him the devil continually. One day he talked back and told her that in all his life he had never met anyone so mouthy and unreasonable as she was, except that foreman in X—. Then she shrieked, "That's my father!"

As I walked up the street after being fired, I met another striker. I told him where there was a vacancy, but he wasn't interested; in fact, he had the address of a job in his pocket and asked me to take it as the strike benefit was sufficient for his needs and was giving him a good vacation. So within ten minutes I was working as if nothing had happened.

In looking for work, whenever a job ran out, I always visited twenty-five or thirty shops a day. This, of course, gave me five or six times as much chance as the man who only went to four or five places and then went home. One day as I listened to a group of union men chatter about work instead of hunting for it, I heard them say that the employment agency of the Typothetae (non-union employers association) would never give a union man a job, anyhow. Curious to get more data on this theory, I ran right over to the Typothetae. The girl clerk was wreathed in smiles, for a call had just come in for a compositor and as the first candidate the job was mine. No questions were asked of me about the union.

One day I started at seven in the morning, determined to find a job before I went home. I thought: "Just suppose I were a poor married man and had to have some money, I'll bet I could land a job today." I walked to about thirty shops before evening. Then I showed up on the Post, then the Herald and finally the American, in case they needed an extra man for the night. Sure enough, at nine P.M. after a fourteen-hour search, I was at work on the Hearst paper setting ads.

At one place after awhile a colored man said: "DeMar, are you any relation to the runner?" "Yes," I replied, "I'm the fellow who used to." "Aw gwine," he grinned, "DeMar's a decent kind of a fellow."

But all this chasing after work and changing shops, while it didn't cost me much money, was certainly broadening to my all-around experience, yet it was more tiresome than running many, many marathons. Although still in good health, at the end of three months of this changing around I was rather tired and thin. At this time I applied for sick insurance. After a medical examination I was told to withdraw my application so that I could truthfully say I had never been rejected, and it would be much easier to get insurance somewhere else. In other words, they were telling me as courteously as possible that I was a poor risk. Several years later after some marathon stunts they laughed with me about it. Finally, in January, 1921, it was a relief to land a steady situation with Joe Miller in Medford. He had a country shop, but paid Boston wages, and did good work. I took to riding my bicycle from Melrose to Medford and back and thus saved time and car fare.

Early in April on one of our overnight trips to a cottage in North Reading, which the Melrose scouts owned, I had over fifteen boys. This was too large a group. Since we had shelter it was to be expected that there'd be no rain. It was a warm night so several boys slept on the roof. But before morning they had kicked a hole in the tar paper. Wishing to be sure we had left the cottage right for the other troops, on April 19, 1921 I rode my bicycle up and repaired the damage.

On reading the papers the next morning I was delighted to find that Frank Zuna, who had won the Brockton Marathon in 1915, and with whom I had become well acquainted at the Interallied Games, had won the B.A.A. Not only that, but he had broken Mike Ryan's record by nearly three minutes. On the Olympic trip the summer before with Mike Ryan as marathon coach, Zuna had not been able to prove his condition satisfactorily, so had not been allowed to start in the big event. For Zuna now to break the cherished record of the one who had considered him mediocre seemed to me like a reasonable athletic revenge. Zuna always interested me. At preparation for the Interallied Games in order to be on the mile squad it was necessary to do the distance under five minutes. As Zuna could do this he didn't bother to try ten miles. Why run ten miles when you could have all the privileges of the squad by doing just one? And when Zuna went places he usually wore his tracksuit for underwear and jammed his track shoes in his back pants pockets. Later on the trip to Paris in 1924 he just took a small plumber's tool bag with a towel, razor, etc. in it. The marathon record had passed from an Irishman to a Bohemian, from one who capitalized on its possession to one who thought no more of it than he did of a good meal.

There was to be a mile race at the Melrose celebration on July 4, 1921. I practiced from the first of June by running easy miles, which was several laps around the knoll at Ell Pond. I won this mile in four minutes and forty-seven and three-fifths seconds in one of the two or three times that I've ever run under five minutes.

In the fall of 1921 I dropped my Sunday School class for a year. I put all my attention, aside from earning my living, on the scouts, and had a loyal, active troop who were keen for competition of any kind, and willing to do a certain amount of scout work.

During late November of that year we had a big sleet storm which broke the trees and made the streets almost impassable. I could not ride my bike to work, and the trolley would have taken hours from Melrose to Medford, so I jogged to work and home again for the first time in years. The four and one half miles each way didn't tire me at all. And I had more time to practice running then if I wanted. There was no overtime at the shop, and the foreman at Millers was Bob Campbell, a regular athletic fan with plenty of encouragement for all sports. So my rest from marathon running was about to end.

1910- Clarence DeMar wearing a
North Dorchester Athletic Association uniform.

1927- Nearing the finish line of DeMar's 5th Boston victory.

1928- DeMar's 6th Boston Marathon victory.

Enjoying soup after a Boston victory.

1930- Hans Oldag, Ford Clark and Clarence DeMar.

1930- Boston's "Heartbreak Hill"

1930- DeMar wins his 7th Boston Marathon victory.
(DeMar was actually 42 for his 7th victory)

1930- Honored after 7th Boston Marathon Victory.

1930- With Willie Kyronen, who placed 2nd behind DeMar.

Margaret and Clarence DeMar in the print shop.

1937- Clarence running with Dorothy and Robert.

1937- (left to right) Charles, Margaret, Betty, Clarence, Barbara, Robert, Dorothy.

1937- Clarence with sons Charles and Robert.

1937- Clarence and wife Margaret in Keene, NH.

1937- Clarence with twin daughters
Babara and Betty.

1937- Cutting wood at home in New Hampshire.

1937- One of the twins with dad's newest trophy.

1937- Clarence with oldest son Robert.

1937- Margaret and Clarence DeMar with twin daughters
Barbara and Betty.

1937- Clarence, daughter Dorothy and son Robert.

Finishing with no runner in sight behind him.

c.1940- Running a once rural section of the B.A.A.

c.1940- Clarence speaks with Ellison "Tarzan" Brown
of Westerly, RI.

The oldest and youngest runners of the 1953
Boston Marathon.

1953- The crowd erupts as DeMar finishes
his 32nd Boston Marathon in at age 64.

Clarence ran his last Boston Marathon in
1954 at the age of 65 with a time of 3:58:34.

Photos courtesy of the Boston Public Library,
Leslie Jones Collection

Chapter 9
The Big Surprise

Before New Year's Day, 1922, I had decided to run the B.A.A. marathon again. I followed my usual practice of slow training. I would run the four and one half miles to Medford and back four or five times a week and ride by bicycle the other times. I'd also take a couple of evenings and do two or three laps around Spot Pond (about five miles to a lap). I found that I could stand more work and get less fatigued than ever before. That season I didn't seem to overdo the training slightly so that I'd have to rest up two or three days. All winter I had but one slight cold and in those days I was apt to have a couple. I felt very confident that I was pretty good, but I never ran faster than eight miles per hour. Just once, several weeks before April 19, I went out to Wellesley Square and ran as fast as I could to the finish, then jogged to Melrose. I did the fourteen miles from Wellesley to the finish in one hour, eighteen minutes. I figured that I could run from Ashland to Wellesley in an hour and then by calling on my reserves and with the excitement could do the last fourteen miles pretty close to what I had done in practice. That is just about the way it came out, too.

But before the race as in 1911, when I won, and contrasted to 1910 and 1917 when I ran and did not win, I dreamed that I won. I began to be curious about these dreams and was a little superstitious at heart, although on the surface everyone knows better. This dream did give me confidence, even if it was nonsense, and I needed it, for no man outside of Bob Campbell thought I had any chance. My loyal scouts, however, took it as a matter of fact that I might win. There wasn't any favorable comment from sport's writers, except that John Hallahan of the Globe said I had the spirit to fit in there somewhere. Yet in the last previous marathon in which I had started, the Brockton in 1917, I had won and broken the record!

After an early breakfast at home, consisting of prunes, oatmeal, eggs and toast, my brother Bob took me out to the start of the race. We stopped at Framingham and had our own fresh eggs cooked, and with more toast and milk this completed the eating.

Bob Campbell, my foreman, rode the bicycle and was by far the best I ever had. From his wide appreciation of sports he acted both hopeful and helpful. In those days the police protection against the growing auto menace had not been perfected as now, so Bob used his militia military training language to clear the road and he did a pretty good job.

While going through Wellesley very near the leaders and running on the right-hand sidewalk, an open car made a quick left turn and just grazed me. Furious at even a trivial thwarting of my big object I aimed a blow at the driver, but owing to the movement of the car, got the man in the rear seat in the ribs. He was surprised, but whether the car turned to investigate I never knew, for the reaction was enough to make me run even faster for a couple of miles.

As we approached Auburndale I had quite a battle with an Indian runner named Smoke from Canada. Up over the Newton Hills I had the lead, with Jimmie Henigan, not yet able to run a marathon, racing me every yard. Just before Lake Street I shook him as expected and came down the home stretch all alone.

From the Boston and Albany Bridge on, the officials, including my old friend, George Brown, were very excited, urging me to make a new record. I had my times and distances down pretty well and felt I would get it without so much fuss. However, after all, I was only some seconds ahead of Zuna's record record of 2:18:57 from the year before. My time was 2:18:10. This still stands as the record for the old course. Ritola, who was to become such a great 5- and 10-miler for Finland, was second, and the best Zuna could do was eighth.

My victory created a big surprise. Athletic coaches each had a paragraph in the Boston Post giving their opinion of how I had done it- Several of them said that they thought brain work had something to do with it. That brains enough to concentrate as much as possible on one's physical and mental ability during the race is necessary in order to be a winner.).

After the victory I got an invitation to speak in Tremont Temple to the Brotherhood and also at Athol, Massachusetts. I also had many requests to come to receptions, and show myself as a curiosity, I suppose. My own church had a reception and supper for me with the Troop as guests.

Then the City of Melrose seemed to feel that I was a stable enough citizen to merit a blow-out Boy Scout officials and others held a tag day to raise money to give me a present. I was embarrassed by this and it was a toss up as to whether I'd stop it or let the show go on. By a hairline decision I decided to go through the ordeal. As I've told Les Pawson and Tarzan Brown since, "The first celebration is the hardest." Beside the banquet they presented me with a beautiful watch and chain and listened to my speech about how it was done.

But all this celebrating and going places took time and energy. I didn't do much running, and my scout troop suffered from neglect of the extra evening's practice and lost a couple of meets. However, in one way the troop benefited materially by my victory, for I turned over to them the one hundred dollars which the Boston Globe paid me for a three-thousand word feature article I stayed up all night April 19th to write at their request.

Throughout the following winter I continued my practice and was getting along about the same when early in February while running down Fulton Street, Medford, between high banks of snow, a big dog obstructed my path and made a tremendous lunge at me. With my sneakers I kicked at him and strove to get past. At once someone sprang from behind and biffed me in the face, opening a gash on my upper lip from which blood rushed. Two men confronted me. One said, "Kick my dog, will you? He was barking a welcome to me." An infection set in from the gash on my face and I was quite sick with erysipelas for ten days. Those days with the two I lost after camping in 1916, and one in college after indulging in two sodas for a nickel, make up the thirteen days I have lost because of sickness since 1903 when I graduated from grammar school.

So in the middle of February 1923, I had to begin my training over again. Although weak after ten days in bed I quickly began to pick up and was in fair shape April 19th, except for a cold, which I was doctoring. I didn't have any dream about winning and was beginning to wonder, subconsciously, if I was going to lose. The night before the race I got a special delivery letter from a fellow named Miller of Greenfield, Massachusetts. Miller wrote that I'd probably think him queer, but he had always been interested in athletics and had had a clear dream the last night. The dream was that I had won, but Zuna in a dark suit (interallied running pants) had threatened near the finish. He hoped I'd watch Zuna.

At the start I was as uneasy as usual, trying to get everything just right. This time no one nagged me to do something or not to, and that was a help. Just a couple of minutes before the gun, in restlessly adjusting my trunks, socks and shoes, because it takes so little to make or prevent a blister or a chafe, I had the sudden idea of pinning my socks to my shoes with safety pins. That is

how my custom of using safety pins for garters originated.
It was a very lucky move this time, too, as events proved.
This 1923 race was much harder than the year before.
It was hot, but I was not yet so old that I needed heat to
kill off youth. With my winter's illness from the dog
episode, and my present cold, I was very tired at
Framingham and felt like stopping. However, I didn't
have that habit, so I continued. Finally, I worked up with
and past all the leaders except "Whitey" Michelson.
Whitey was a newcomer and a protégé of Bill Kennedy.
We were to see a lot more of him later. Michelson and I
had quite a duel up past Lake Street to Chestnut Hill. I
had no sooner got rid of Michelson than a worse thing
happened to me. Just before Cleveland Circle an auto hit a
bicycle, which hit my foot, thus pulling the shoe off the
heel. The safety pins, which I had put in as a last minute
nervous guess, held the shoe from flying away. But it was
an awkward situation. At once the people in cars, seeing
the difficulty, began to give advice. "Stop and fix it,"
shouted one; "Take the shoe off and run barefooted,"
suggested another. True to one item of my philosophy of
life not to take advice least I become like the "chaff which
the wind driveth away" I ignored the yelling and let well
enough alone, so long as it didn't get any worse, and just
shuffled along, being careful each step not to lose the
shoe. It slowed me a bit and greatly increased the
uncertainty and nervous strain from having to be
conscious and careful of every other step. But Zuna, who
had moved into second place, and was threatening as
Miller's dream had outlined, didn't gain very much. The
time was more than five minutes slower than the year
before, partly due to the heat. However, I had sweated out
all my cold. So that is one way to cure a cold sometimes,
just run a marathon on a hot day!

For the 1923 victory I had transferred from the colors
of the Dorchester Club to the Melrose Post, number
ninety of the American Legion. It seemed much better to
represent something in Melrose. The post always honored
me for marathon victories far more than I deserved, or

wished. After this win they raised money to send me to their national convention in San Francisco in October. While out there I ran a couple of small races at the Berkeley oval and met Bill Churchill who was to come east next year and make the Olympic Marathon team. At the Grand Canyon I saved seven dollars by walking down the trail and back instead of hiring a burro. With my street clothes on I took slightly more time for the trip than old man Weston's record. En route I also stopped at Cincinnati to see all my relatives, whom I had not seen for twenty-four years.

During 1923, unlike '22, when I entered no competition, I ran several races. I made a fair showing but did not go into it seriously enough to endanger my marathon pace.

While practicing the following winter I jumped over a snowdrift in such a way that my back and hip became lame. I rubbed on all the liniments, but I was still unable to run as before. While in this condition I accepted my first invitation to the Baltimore marathon. I remember saying to Zuna before the race, "You may win here, but I'll win at Boston."

From the beginning I was outclassed in the race, first by Michelson, and then by Zuna, who won. I got third, eight or nine minutes back.

Wishing to remedy my lameness for the B.A.A., I tried an osteopath for the first time. Sure enough, in two treatments he had my back and hip as good as ever. Since then, as I have become older, I have had other lamenesses in my back and hips which osteopaths could not cure so easily. Sometimes even a dozen treatments doesn't make it right, but they help a lot. I suppose that fifty years ago, before they had osteopathy, my victorious marathon days would have ended with the minor accident of the winter of 1923-4.

Being well again, I practiced a great deal, cautiously and without exertion, aiming to gain the victory on April 19. I didn't allow any suggested engagements to turn me aside from the main objective. I dreamed of victory and so the string of coincidences of dreams coming true was to be unbroken. Sunday afternoon, the day before the race, I was speaking to a young people's meeting in Wilmington, Massachusetts. During the talk I told them that I would win the next day, which may have been more of a challenge to myself than a feeling of confidence.

This 1924 marathon was lengthened to be 26 miles, 385 yards to correspond with the Olympic distance. I ran with great confidence and felt that I had a grasp of the distance and my competitors' abilities from the first. At the finish, which I did just under 2:30, I was several minutes ahead of Chuck Mellor who had run away from me at Coblenz.

It was about this time that Miss Margaret Ilsley who was to become my wife years later, asked me to teach some boys at a Methodist Mission in the North End of Boston, in which she was interested. I continued this for over five years and certainly enjoyed the dark little fellows and learned to appreciate their ability at music and their eagerness to lead the prayers.

This mission work, however, was just coincident with the "Big Surprise." The "Big Surprise" consisted in winning three B.A.A. marathons in a row, after being out of competition for years, and when everyone had said no one would ever win two. The 1924 victory made me a member of the Olympic team about to sail for Paris. Probably that trip had better be described in the next chapter, for while I managed to do well, there was nothing surprising about my showing.

Chapter 10
The 1924 Olympics

There were six runners and one substitute on the 1924 Olympic Marathon team. They were: Chuck Mellor of Chicago, Frank Zuna of Newark, New Jersey, Frank Wendling of Buffalo, William Churchill of San Francisco, the American Finns—Carl Linder and Ralph Williams— of Quincy, Massachusetts, and myself. Presumably Williams was the sub, since he had made the poorest showing in the try out, but that remained to be seen.

After my disastrous experience with the Olympic organization in 1912 and with the history of the boys' troubles in 1920 still ringing in my ears, I determined to get better conditions for success in 1924. Lawson Robertson of Pennsylvania was head coach.

So at the Baltimore race early in March I nailed Robertson, saying that if I went to Paris I wouldn't put up with any nonsense from coaches. He cordially agreed, saying that he had had cross-country runners at Pennsylvania who did better alone. I also wrote to Mike Ryan then at Colby, who was again to be the Marathon coach, that he must not bother me on the trip. Finally, he replied that there would be no trouble.

We marathoners were to go over early, and preparatory to starting met at a hotel in New York. There, as I might have expected, was an atmosphere of official domination, or just plain officiousness. We were told that the coach's word was final, that we'd train together and be one big, happy family and like it. In righteous indignation I interrupted to say that it had already been agreed that I was to train alone, when I wished. Robertson said, "Shh! We don't mean you. We'll keep our promise, but you'll destroy the confidence of these men in their coach." I wondered how much confidence Zuna, Linder and Mellor had after 1920. At that time, not having any marathon runner's association and the other men not having asked me to fight for them, I did not feel called on to demand more than my own rights.

The training proceeded as was to be expected. Ryan rode in a taxi and hollered at the other six. "Altogether there, not too fast. Say, you've only been out forty-five minutes and will have to go further!" I ran as I pleased, usually for a long time in a leisurely way. Sometimes I took a day off and went swimming or sightseeing. Just two or three times I ran with the group for the fun of it. Since there was an extra man on the squad they were continually on edge with the fear of not making good. Two weeks before the contest we ran a practice 15-mile on a grass track. I don't recall all the places at the finish, but I was first, Wendling second, and Linder was well up.

Then the authorities pulled the prize boner. When the entries were finally sent in, Williams was entered, and Linder, who had made the team at Boston and then had shown well at our informal fifteen-mile race, was dropped. I have always wondered just which of the Olympic officials wanted to gamble on a youngster like Williams winning the big race as a dark horse, knowing that while Linder would run a good race, he had no chance of winning. But Linder had won a place as a regular member of the team, and he was still in good condition. Williams had not shown that he was any better than seventh man and a sub. This trick destroyed any hope and morale that any of the men had left.

When the race came, as one would expect in Paris in July, it was hot. As usual for Olympic marathons, the run was 13 miles out and back. The course was flat, with macadam road most of the way, and some cobblestones in the villages. The French authorities ruled that the autos were to have one half the road and the runners the other. This rule was respected by all parties, and worked very well. The best anyone could do in the heat was to slow up from the usual ten-mile-per-hour marathon pace and plod along, occasionally giving battle to a Frenchman, an Italian, a Finn, or someone from South America, for a better position. It was certainly grueling work racing under the hot sun, and it required all one's determination and patriotism to keep from quitting or at least slowing down to a walk. One thing that always gives me comfort in a race of this kind when I feel very tired is the thought that my competitors probably feel just as bad, or worse.

About three miles from the finish an Englishman shouted to me, "Take the sidewalk, take the sidewalk." I continued in the street as was to be expected. He said, "The bally runner has no brains." Hot as it was, I advised the Englishman to go to a much hotter place. The excitement of the altercation reacted on me as usual, so that I ran better to the finish. Stenroos from Finland won by a wide margin in two hours and forty-two minutes; an Italian was second; and I came third, just back of second man. They put up a big Finnish flag on the center pole and smaller flags of Italy and America on the right and left for second and third. This was the first time since 1912 when the neglected Strobino was third that we had had an American flag up for the marathon.

After being forced to train en masse with someone in authority to bother, the next American was sixteenth, about three miles back of me.

All the Americans finished somewhere, away back, except Williams, the man the officials had fired Linder to make room for. Williams dropped out.

Before the race we runners had agreed that whoever made the best showing should draw up a paper telling the Olympic officials what we thought of their coaching arrangements. So I had that privilege and all signed my document, except Wendling, who considered it truthful, but discourteous. Before handing it in I read the paper to Ryan and asked if there was any reason why I should not hand it in. It stated conditions pretty frankly, and we all pledged ourselves never to go to the games again with any coach in charge. For once Mike said nothing.

The officials didn't comment directly, although they abolished the marathon coach for the next Olympiad, 1928, when I was again a member. Colonel Thompson had some words of consolation for me for not winning, sort of implying that that was what I was displeased about. But he was mistaken. Getting third in the Olympics was very satisfactory to me and I considered it a successful, if not a victorious, race.

Alonzo Stagg, the great football coach, was present at the games in some capacity. One day he casually asked me what had been the matter with the other runners. I said that the answer was simple. They had had to put up with a coach, while I had forced an agreement before leaving that I was to train myself. Mr. Stagg smiled incredulously. With all his experience and broad sympathy, yet as a professional coach he evidently could not conceive of an Olympic coach being a nuisance.

When Ryan sent in his official report he blamed the failure of the other members of the team on the heat, and the fear of the men of coming to harm, after witnessing the cross-country run in which there had been collapsing and other disasters. As for me, he said I could just as well have won the race only I was too yellow and afraid to exert myself. I often laugh about that and think it a compliment to have been called good enough to win an Olympic.

On such trips one spends quite a lot of money out of his own pocket and much of it could be paid by the Olympic Committee if they had it. For instance, we marathoners had paid ten dollars for our visa on passports (on account of going over early). We decided to make the committee pay it back. They didn't intend to, but after the boys had called at their office a few times in a taxi, the taxi bill being charged to the boarding house for which the committee was paying, they were glad to settle up.

We were gone about ten weeks and the loss of wages was beginning to be felt, so I managed to swap my passage home for third class and some money. It took a lot of argument with the financial part of the Olympic Committee to get this cash. I couldn't see what difference it made to them how I came back so long as it cost them the same, but they said that it was a dangerous precedent to give any athlete money for his passage home as the news would get around and many who were not responsible would demand it, waste all the cash, and then be stranded, with the American consuls demanding that the committee send the boys home. However, by persistence, I got what I was after and I doubt if the athletes were any more irresponsible than the officials.

Coming back in the steerage was a novel experience, and I'd do it again to save one hundred dollars. There were various examinations and a vaccination. There was a long line at the customs but only a superficial examination of luggage. After awaiting my turn the man said, "What, you are the fellow that did all this distance running. You ought to have come up front at once." But people will agree that no athlete who thus habitually imposed on people because of his fame, would have the opportunity long.

On returning from the Olympics I ran a number of smaller races, making a fair showing. At this time my amateur standing changed from absolute to relative. Up to this point I had never made a cent for any race, had spent small sums from my pocket for minor races, and made sacrifices in wages to go to the Olympic Games and some to go to the coast to the Legion Convention. Now I began to get offers to run in meets with surprising expenses. Still a little scrupulous, I merely hired a car to take some of my boys to the races to give them an outing.

It was in the fall of 1924 that I volunteered to become scoutmaster of Troop nine, Maplewood (Malden). I kept this position for five years until going to Keene. With all the time it takes, the scout program is fascinating and Malden had a first-class Council. I enjoyed the work and appreciated the cooperation of fellows like Ralph McElroy and Harry Olson, who were growing leaders themselves, and kept the troop going better than ever after I left.

While I didn't win any marathons in 1925 I did win a big 15-mile on a track in North Cambridge, beating, among others, Stenroos, the Olympic champion. In the B.A.A. Chuck Mellor beat me by thirty-seven seconds. Then in a marathon at Buffalo on May 30, I was only third with Wendling and Michelson winning. The first Port Chester race was held October 12, 1925. Michelson and I had a close battle most of the way, with him winning by a couple of minutes. His time that day for the full distance was under two hours and thirty minutes, which would have won any Olympic marathon.

During that summer I ran quite a number of shorter races too, and by hard work could usually get a prize. In one race in Quincy a young runner ran by my side for five miles than suddenly quit. Afterwards he told me in the dressing room, "You plank your feet down so hard, and make so much work of running, that it made me nervous and I had to quit!"

My job in Medford ran out early in the summer of 1925 and I had to change around a little before I got settled in Cambridge for a year and a half at the "Warren Publications." Then I had another spell of short jobs before settling at the Jamaica Plain Journal for two-and-a-half years before going to Keene. It was during one of these shifts that I picked up a job for a week at a shop near the North Station. They merely asked my experience and whether I belonged to the Union but not my name. After five days the errand boy said, "You make me think of Clarence DeMar. I saw him working on the American one night." I said, "Isn't that a coincidence, what is the resemblance—a kind of a lean hungry look?" But he finally decided that I was the runner.

When the B.A.A. came around in 1926, we were pleased to have Stenroos, the Olympic champion, as an entry. Some people thought he and I would have a close battle, but barring accident or discouragement Stenroos was a lot better than I. However, the honors were to go to neither of us that day. Johnny Miles, maritime 10-mile champion, with his heart set on a great victory, and pictures of Stenroos and DeMar in his pocket, and not spoiled by any advice or urging, just practiced when he felt like it all winter, and came down to run the fastest marathon of all time.

At ten miles, which he and Stenroos did in close to fifty-five minutes, they were two minutes ahead. These two had a great battle as far as Lake Street, where Stenroos weakened and Miles romped in to win in two hours twenty-five minutes and forty seconds. Stenroos was one-fifth second better than my 1924 time, just under two hours and thirty minutes and I was a couple of minutes back in third place. This record of Miles was so phenomenal that people thought the course must be short, so it was surveyed and found to be just one hundred seventy-six yards shy. Any marathoner can do one hundred seventy-six yards in thirty-five or forty seconds, so Miles' corrected time would not have been over two hours twenty-six minutes and twenty seconds, a mark that has never been approached in any marathon, anywhere. There have been two or three cases where runners have done under two hours and thirty minutes, but never anything like that. However, I have no doubt that sometime it will be done, for Les Pawson without a head wind in 1933 could have been two or three minutes under two hours and thirty minutes, and if in 1936 the Indian, Tarzan Brown, could have kept up for the last five miles the way he ran for the first twenty-one, he would have done nearly as well as Miles. But up to date many of us are very sure that Miles' 1926 B.A.A. was the fastest marathon ever run.

Getting third to such a pair as Miles and Stenroos was not a slip and I was soon to win five marathons in a row in a year, which is the best I've ever done. These five victories were the Baltimore race the middle of May, 1926, the Sesqui-Centennial at Philadelphia, early in June; the Port Chester, October 12th; the Baltimore again in March, 1927; and the B.AA., April 19, 1927. I lost the sixth try at Buffalo, on May 30, 1927, to Bricker of Toronto by less than thirty seconds.

A description of these five victories may furnish interesting reading to fans, as well as present and future runners. The N.E.A.A.U. sent me to the Baltimore marathon, which was to be the national championship that year. At the race Michelson was my logical close rival. A carload of his friends from Stamford, Connecticut, had accompanied him. I have always been sure that a carload of friends, or a girl, is a big handicap for a runner at a marathon. They are almost sure to be a distraction and victors require great concentration in these days of keen competition. But this car of friends helped some by having plenty of water, which Michelson much needed. The natives, officials, and small boys were not doing their usual generous job. Once I asked a youngster on a bike for a drink. He said, "I've got some tea that belongs to Mike Lynch, you may have some." I declined on the general principle that I never drink anything in competition that I have not first tried in practice. Afterwards Mike said, "The little cuss gave it all to someone, I never got any." Another small boy said, "I'll get you some water." Half a mile further, there he was pumping at a farmhouse fifty yards back of the road and yelling, "Here's your water, mister." But I never detour while racing. After going half way in the hot sun without water, my mouth and throat was in pretty tough shape. Then Michelson's friends offered me a drink. I had noticed they had plenty of liquid but was too proud to ask a rival for water.

I accepted the water with great thanks and for about the next ten miles, until I got quite a lead on their man, they gave me frequent drinks. Michelson finished second and I told his friends that possibly he'd have won if they hadn't given me the water. They laughed and said they had offered it to a lot of runners but no one except me had trusted them. So I was National Marathon Champion the first time, Mellor having won the honor the previous year when it was established. Because my throat was parched before I was given water, I had to whisper for two days.

Next came the Sesqui-Centennial marathon at Philadelphia. Early in the week I had memorized the course from a map, then had rehearsed it the night before. As a result everything seemed almost as familiar as at the B.A.A. Among the runners in this race was Stenroos. I managed to stay with him for about an hour when we struck some freshly tarred road, then some loose gravel. After one's shoes had become stuck with the tar and then began to pick up gravel it was very annoying. The Finns usually say nothing, but this time Stenroos made a remark in Finnish (he may have been cursing the fly-paper) and then quit. I won by one-half mile, with Michelson second again. There were only a few people in the stadium to see the finish. The prize was a huge hammered silver trophy. Someone seeing it remarked, "No wonder the Sesqui went broke."

In the fall came the Port Chester marathon again. Some Boston reporter in New York found me before the race and bought me a big steak dinner. I felt very grateful to him, until during the race he did much more than the cost of the steak's worth of damage with his attempts at coaching. But Michelson was off form so I won in much slower time than the year before when I was second.

Then I had all winter to prepare for the big B.A.A. and Baltimore marathons. Meanwhile Stenroos had returned to Finland. When asked his opinion of American runners he said he thought I'd be good in a couple of years. (Stenroos is a couple of years my senior!)

The Baltimore race came in March this time. About a week before going down I tripped over a rough spot in the sidewalk and wounded my knee. It got a little infected and I could hardly walk, but strange to say I could run all right. The doctor advised boric acid solution to take out the inflammation and I kept it wet all the way to Baltimore. Michelson had been aiming to turn the tables on me after four straight defeats, and he came very near doing it. After a neck and neck struggle for the whole distance, with the crowds seeming to favor Michelson, I won by less than one hundred yards. It took a lot more exertion than I generally care to use, but one reason I did so this time was because I had a talk to give at the "Y" in Washington that evening and I figured the speech would go better after a victory. Also, I had casually mentioned to someone that I was going to win and I wanted to make good.

Less than a month after this I again had the B.A.A. Meanwhile I had another accident, dropping the sheet metal bottom of a Poco Proof Press on my big toe and jamming it badly. It hadn't recovered when the managers of the Cathedral run asked me to enter. I obliged. From a low mark I got twenty-sixth. Some commented sneeringly that I was probably lying down for the B.A.A. next week. But people who know running realize that because you finish away back in handicap races is no sign you are lying down. That is one thing handicaps are for: to give a lot of not-so-goods a chance to be in front. Besides, in an amateur race, if anyone wants to take it a little easy, he has that right; for he is not paid, but is running for the fun of it.

Before the B.A.A., for the first time in three years, I dreamed of victory. This was encouraging but the odds seemed against me, for Miles was down to repeat. I started at a good pace and was with the leaders through Framingham. I was racing Miles that day. In all my other marathons I've raced against time, but this race it was

Miles, the fastest marathoner ever. I just wouldn't let Miles keep the lead but would spurt ahead every quarter mile. It was hot, so hot that the tar was like flypaper in certain places. So it was not surprising that before we reached Natick, Miles, from the frozen North, had quit. I'd already beaten my man but as was to be expected had put myself in difficulty. In trimming Miles I had become very tired myself and I still had twenty miles to go!

Continuing with keen tension and watching everything possible, I always turned my head slightly as any motor cop came roaring from the rear. Whereupon an official from Melrose, wishing me well, but with poor judgment, yelled, "Tell him not to turn his head that way; the motorcycle won't hit him." Even if the rushing cops only hit me once in a thousand times, still it was worth inclining my head every time to be prepared to jump aside that once!

Before the hills I got a fair lead with Karl Koski second. Up through the Newtons I was very, very tired and thirsty. Officials and others helped with water. I found a car with a pail of ice water on the running board. First I took a few swallows of the cold liquid. It refreshed me, and I had often drunk ice water in practice. So every time I could find that car I drank a lot. It helped save the day for me. This by no means implies that runners should drink ice water in a marathon. It simply means that in exceptional circumstances one may do exceptional things, so on a torrid day in a marathon it may be tried cautiously.

I finally won in rather slow time. While very tired, I probably was never in danger of collapsing except at Kenmore, when I felt very dizzy and faint. In all my running career I have never collapsed, so I feel fairly secure; but this was the nearest to a catastrophe I ever came, and the finish less than a mile away. A slower pace for a hundred yards saved me.

Naturally after a three-year lapse from B.A.A. victories, this one brought lots of publicity. Early the next morning a newspaper reporter wanted a picture of me running for the train. Then he took the same train and asked the fare to Boston. On being told it was twenty-six cents he said, "It'll be more than that when I send in my bill." He'd do all right for a "relative" amateur. At the shop on India Street he took pictures of me punching the clock and going to work. Finally, I settled down to typesetting, but at ten A.M. he was back apologetically explaining that the editor of the Boston America was a nut, but he must have a picture of my feet. I said that in such cases I supposed any pair of hoofs would be OK. Who'd know whether they were mine or not? He exclaimed, "For the other papers, yes, but never for the American." So I removed my footwear and he took some exposures, which were all over the sports page that evening.

Throughout the latter half of the twenties I ran my scouts, Sunday School class and mission class in the North End with regularity and fair success. I often gave trophies and watches to keep up interest. For two years in succession my class of high school boys at the Baptist Sunday School in Melrose had such a close contest for giving the best talks on each lesson for the year that I gave four watches instead of the one promised.

I remember, also, one scout in Malden who amassed a great number of merit badges to get points to win a watch two years in succession. I'm not sure that there wasn't some over-emphasis on advancement to get the prize, yet it did no harm and he did one hundred times as much work for the watch as I.

If I really began to slip as a runner in the foil of 1927, I made a vigorous kick for several years and had my share of victories. In the spring of 1928 I won both the Providence-Boston forty-four mile run and the BAA., which was the National Championship and the Olympic try out. In both these races the odd coincidence of dreams held good. Before the forty-four mile I got a letter from my former scout, Bill Benedict, then a student and a runner at the University of New Hampshire, saying that he had had a clear dream of my having a hard race as for as Wrentham and then winning as I pleased. After running side by side with Dodge of Melrose as far as Wrentham Square I thought if the dream was good for anything I ought to shake this fellow. Sure enough, in crossing the bridge a few yards further, he dropped back and I won by two or three miles.

Then, for the last time in the 1928 B.A.A., the dream and the victory coincided in the same year. After that the coincidence of dreams and victory stopped. Dreams which people reported before the 1929 B.A.A. predicted my victory. I couldn't believe it, since my condition was not right. However, I did win in 1930. Since then dreams seem to indicate another B.A.A. victory sometime, but they must be just the ramblings of a tired brain, for how can a man of nearly fifty beat the best youth in the country?

However, it was a most unusual coincidence that from 1910 through 1928 in ten starts that dreams should have told of the six victories and been silent for the four defeats, and that in one of these cases the dream was by a total stranger. Also, there is that unusual dream of the college boy about the forty-four mile, foretelling the exact point where I'd take the lead. But then he was interested in running and knew the game.

During these years from 1924 through 1929, I kept in excellent health and worked steady as a compositor. Unlike my experience in 1914, when it took me forty hours to prepare a fifteen-minute talk, I now could make a speech without preparation, so that speeches now were easier than marathons.

Chapter 11
Speaking of Running

Public speaking and Marathon running don't necessarily go hand in hand. But after the 1922 B.A.A. race I was invited to make a speech which let me in for fifteen years of platform appearances in schools, churches, clubs, Y.M.C.A.'s, jails and C.C.C. camps. For one who usually doesn't talk very much I seem to have given my vocal chords quite a bit of exercise. The funny part about this speech-making is that I have been invited back to the same place in several instances.

One of the most thrilling occasions was when I first spoke before a High School. This was in Berlin, N. H., in the fall of 1924. The filled hall, the enthusiasm of youth, the eagerness with which they listened to anecdotes about running, and their applause at the finish of a talk that was not too long, quickly convinced me that my favorite audience is a junior or Senior High School.

There is one other place besides a school where I have always been sure of a well-filled hall, and that is in jails! Twice I have spoken before the State prison at Charlestown and once before the Reformatory at Concord. At Charlestown I thought the audience was a little cool. There was something of the atmosphere of a church service. But I was invited back a couple of other times. After the talk, one prisoner spoke to me because his brother was a famous half-miler. At least, I've never found any well-known runners there. And it is a claim of many that no good printers ever go to jail. So as a runner and a printer perhaps I'm fairly safe!

The audience at Concord seemed quite enthusiastic. This was not a church service, but an entertainment. As the rest of the show was by professionals I felt that I'd be an anti-climax, but as I was fresh from a B.A.A. victory they gave me a fine welcome.

I guess most of my speeches have been fairly satisfactory. An American audience is rather docile and probably wouldn't say so even if they were disgusted with me. However, the only complaints that I have had have been that either I didn't tell enough about my races or else I didn't talk long enough.

Besides the church talk on "The Race of Life" published in the Christian Herald, I had another talk on "What Determines the Winner" which a reporter caught and printed in the Boston Globe. More recently I had a talk on "The Greatest Difficulty in Marathon Running." This was published in the April, 1936, American Legion Monthly, under the title, "They mean well, but-"

Since one of these talks explains in as few words as possible why I believe athletics can help make for a balanced life, I want to include it here:

"In school we used to express proportion as 'two is to four as four is to eight'. And the ends, two times eight, balanced the middle, four times four. Now success in marathon running requires a sense of balance and proportion.

"At the outset someone might say that all the publicity and fame that goes with athletic success is out of all proportion to the importance of the achievement and that the one so honored would surely get a swelled head and become socially unbalanced. There is no doubt some danger of this with those of high school age; but after one has reached the maturity of a marathon runner he will

have received so many knocks that all this temporary honor simply balances it.

"In getting ready for the race the most important thing is to do a lot of practice. The amount and speed may vary with individuals, but a great deal must be done. I averaged one hundred miles per week for two months before April 19th. In proportion as the amount of work is increased so more refreshing sleep is necessary to balance this wear and tear on the human machine. With the exception of one or two nights a week, I think it is necessary to spend nine or ten hours in bed each night with eight or nine hours of sleep. This is very difficult when there are so many things going on that one wants to take in, but it is necessary. A man when asked the secret of his living to be nearly one hundred said, 'I sleep nine hours every night.' Someone exclaimed, 'Sleep nine hours every night! Why he never lived one hundred years, he only lived fifty!' But though you only live half your life, you must get plenty of sleep to balance the hard work in training.

"While the running and the sleep are the most important things from my view point, yet from the questions many people ask you'd think the food was. For hogs and cows, agricultural experiment stations have learned that a balance and proper proportions of proteins, carbohydrates and fats is very necessary for the best results in producing pork and beef. However, my experience has been that we humans do not need to be so fussy. While there is still lots to learn, yet, having gone a year on a well-balanced diet with proper calories and found it a lot of bother with no benefit, I'll simply say that according to my present knowledge food is one place where the sense of balance and proportion is not so obvious.

"We humans seem to be on higher level than hogs, so far as food is concerned, at least. Very likely the balance is there in a simple home diet, so well that if we fussed with it we wouldn't make the proportion much better and we might take all the joy out of eating.

"There is also a sense of proportion necessary in the relationship between marathon running and the other affairs of life. Someone has said: 'All work and no play makes Jack a dull boy,' and som one else, 'All play and no work makes him an awful dumbbell.' Whether marathon running is work or play, it must be balanced with the proper amount of other interests.

"To show the danger of over specialization there is the story of the boy who was brought up in the far west and learned all about horses, but nothing else. While an infant, his mother died and his father brought him up miles from anywhere, and taught him how to take care of horses to the neglect of everything else. He learned how to feed the animals, how to clean them off, and how to break them in. He learned that if a horse broke his leg he must be shot. He also learned to tell a good horse when he saw it. As a young man he knew as much about horses as anyone, but he didn't know anything else.

"One day his father took him many miles to a train to come east on business. The boy noticed a woman, the first one in his life. 'Dad,' he exclaimed 'What's that?' 'That,' replied dad, 'is a woman. You'll get married to one some day.' 'I want one now,' persisted the son.

"After a few months in the East, sure enough the son got married and returned to the ranch with his wife, leaving his father to complete his business. Some months later the father went home. He found the horses well looked after. That was to be expected for the son understood horses. He was a specialist with those animals.

"'By the way,' said dad, 'How's the wife?' 'Oh,' said the son, 'It's too bad about her. She went out to get a pail of water, fell down and broke her leg, so I had to shoot her.'

"So over-specialization is a very bad thing.

"With me, I have my daily job as a compositor. I also have a troop of scouts and a Sunday School class. These activities keep me from becoming over specialized as a

marathoner. On the other hand, I have to guard against becoming tied up with so many petty activities that I'll become distracted and have nothing left for the race. With my living to earn, my scouts and my class work, I felt I had plenty of interests to prevent my becoming a 'nut' on my race and over-specialized.

"Yes, to be successful in marathoning one must have a sense of proportion between the game and other activities of life.

"There is also a sense of proportion necessary between any selfish momentary joy one may get out of some habit and the main thing he has in mind. There are some things that bring a quick thrill but no permanent success. The runner who would be near the front must have a sense of proportion between the minor 'kick' of self-indulgence, and the bigger joy of success.

"Anyone who obeys these senses of balance and proportion while getting ready will be in good shape for the race. They are: the balance between work and rest; the balance of simple food, but not so stereotyped as with cows and hogs; the balance between the game and other activities; and the sense of proportion between a quick thrill and the main thing he has in mind.

"Then after the race gets under way the runner must gauge his pace in proportion to the distance. Anyone who takes his five or ten-mile pace for a marathon will become very tired before he gets there and will probably not finish. I always have a vision of the distance stretching before me and so measure my endurance, making the pace in proportion to the distance.

"One also needs a sense of proportion as to where his power to go ahead comes from—within or without. I would not deny that some cheering from without helps a little, but don't be deceived into thinking that a gaily decorated running suit, a lot of rub-down, or an exhorting bicycle rider can be more than one part in ten thousand compared to the power to go ahead that is within. A bicycle rider once said, 'You know that runner I had? I exhorted him, begged him, prayed him to go faster, swore

*at him and still he would not do anything but poke along.'
Certainly not; the power to go ahead is within—not
without.*

"*Then a sense of proportion is necessary in case of
minor aches of distress or blisters. If there is distress, why
not endure it as a minor thing compared to the great fame
that is to be yours at the finish? That, of course, does not
mean for anyone to force himself against internal pain
which might be serious. Always slow up for a pain in the
side, until it goes. But for a blister, or an abrasion, or a
sore muscle, just go faster to get the distress over with
quicker!*

"*But not only in running but in much of life is a sense
of balance and proportion necessary. As is to be expected
with anything concerning life, there is something about it
in the Bible. After Saul had become king and had been
sent down to destroy the Amalekites and all their cattle,
he came back with some of their best livestock. Coming
upon the prophet Samuel, Saul said, 'I have done as the
Lord commanded.' 'What then is this lowing of cattle?'
asked Samuel. 'Oh,' said Saul, 'These are just a few of the
best ones I brought back to sacrifice.' 'Listen,' said
Samuel, 'When you were little in your own sight you were
big in the sight of God; but when you became big in your
own sight, you became little in the sight of God; you've
lost your job as king. To obey is better than to sacrifice.'
So we have a sense of proportion between what Saul
thought of himself and what God thought of him; and
between sacrifice and obedience.*

"*Later, in the New Testament is the haranguing of the
Master against the Pharisees who didn't have the right
sense of proportion between the outside and the inside of
the cup; between formalism and love; who couldn't tell
the difference between a beam in their own eyes and a
mote in the other fellows'; and who strain out a gnat, but
swallow a camel. Probably you can find other things in
the Bible about a sense of balance and proportion.*

"In life we can find illustrations. Printing to be tasty and artistic must have the proper balance and proportion. But more important than this proportion in the arts is the proportion in human affairs and relationships. Here is a home where the parents are active in the church and the children are pleasant and helpful to all. Here is another home where the father and mother are equally active in the church but without the same sense of proportion are more insistent on trivial forms. The children are ornery and rebellious. Is there any relationship between the magnifying of details by those in authority and the rebellion of youth?

"It is not easy to keep the proper balance and proportion between work and recreation, between saving and generosity, between being a good fellow and yet being careful not to be walked on, between being enthusiastic about one's religion, and yet being careful not to be fanatical. In some things of life where the proportion is bad a sense of humor will relieve the situation. But on the whole there are great changes to be made if the prayer of millions is to be answered: 'Thy kingdom come.'"

Chapter 12
Slipping?

"He's not slipping; he has already slipped." That's what people sometimes say about any athlete when they mean that he's on the bottom. However, just as it is hard to tell when anyone has reached his peak going up, so it is difficult to tell when anyone has reached the lowest point in a slump. As far as I'm concerned, I'm sure I'm not at the bottom yet, so I'm slipping, and probably will be for a long time unless I get some magic potion to restore youth.

But when did I begin to slip? Not before the war, certainly not before 1922, for that was one of the best races of my career. Not even in 1925 when Mellor beat me by thirty-seven seconds and some small boys spying me riding my bicycle to work the next day shouted: "That's the runner feller, he's riding this morning. Ah, you didn't win, did you? Rah, Rah, Raspberry!" (As much as I've worked with boys, I can't understand what it is in the adolescent mind, which prompts them to the cruelty I am sure they don't really mean.) Neither was I slipping in 1926 when Miles and Stenroos beat me, for right after that I had a series of five big victories.

Perhaps I began to slip in the fall of 1927 when, for the first time in my career, I failed to place in the first three in a marathon when I trained as I pleased. (The

Stockholm Olympics with a twelfth didn't count.) But in October, 1927 at the Port Chester Marathon I only got a fourth and then a month later at Halifax, N. S., after racing Johnny Miles on even terms for 15 miles in the cold rain, I got chilled and tired and had to walk the last ten miles, finishing tenth in three hours and thirty minutes.

Probably my slump was hastened a year or two by a stunt during the summer of 1927 that got me very tired. Somewhere I've read that when anyone gets too tired it takes ten times as long for him to recover as it does if he is just fatigued. I think there is some truth in that. One week in August I raced Saturday, then in the middle of the week raced in Nova Scotia, then the following Saturday I did twelve miles around the track at Topsfield, Mass. Sunday afternoon my friend, Bill Leach of Reading, Mass., was starting a one hundred mile hike to Northfield, Mass., to attend the Christian Endeavor Convention. I also had been invited to attend the convention to speak. It seemed too bad to miss this chance for a trip with Bill, so although I was tired after three races in eight days I went.

We walked to Fitchburg without much adventure, except that the State Police at Lunenburg questioned us pretty closely at one A.M. We slept four or five hours at Fitchburg and resumed our tramp. After the first fifty miles the joy and elasticity was gone and it became a grind. Reaching Warwick in the early evening of Monday, there were a number of people who remembered me as a youngster, out to welcome us with refreshments. We got to Northfield at bedtime. The elapsed time for the one hundred mile trip was about thirty-one hours with some twenty-six hours actual walking.

Bill Leach and I had recovered well enough in a couple of days so that we took in a couple of short races at their field day. But the fatigue lingered and the following Saturday I could do no better than ninth in a ten-mile race at Lynn.

While this one hundred mile hike was so fatiguing that I probably began to slip from this point, yet, even so,

117

I do not regret it and would take the trip over again. I've had enough athletic success so that I wouldn't change any duty or any legitimate pleasure one iota to gain more. The one hundred mile walk was a legitimate pleasure.

I rested up in the early winter and then practiced so that I was able to win first, the 44-mile run from Providence to Boston, and then the B.A.A. as mentioned in Chapter 10. The Providence-Boston race was postponed one week because of a big snowstorm. As I had already asked for the Saturday forenoon off from work the day of the storm, I simply went to Providence and jogged the whole distance for the fun of the practice. The following Saturday I was all ready for the contest. In a 44-mile race to set a winning pace one can slow down twenty-five percent from a marathon. Instead of ten miles per hour, seven-and-one-half is satisfactory. I found that I could run this slower pace indefinitely without the nervous strain of the marathon. And also in the seven-and-one-half mile per hour pace there was no danger or difficulty in eating or drinking freely as I ran. I had previously experimented in the practice run, so knew I could take all the buttermilk and soup I wished en route. This race was sponsored by the Shepherd Stores as an advertising stunt. Besides the regular prize, they gave my scouts, Troop nine, Malden, a bass drum. In the B.A.A. I pulled myself together so that I got a reasonable lead coming over the Newton Hills and maintained it to the end. My old friend Jimmie Henigan, finishing his first B.A.A. after trying nearly a generation, was a good second and Joie Ray, running his first long one after a wonderful career as a miler, was third.

The following month I went to New York to run the Long Beach marathon. Ray, recovered from the bad blisters of April 19, won this handily, and the best I could do was seventh. Yes, rapidly approaching my fortieth birthday on June seventh, I was undoubtedly slipping from the natural assurance with which I had always been able to finish first, second, or third in marathons.

On the 1928 Olympic marathon team besides Henigan, Ray and myself were: Harvey Frick of New York, Bill Agee of Baltimore, and Whitey Michelson of Stamford, Conn. Our protest in 1924 had borne fruit and there was no coach or trainer this time, but just a manager, a man named Sullivan from New York. There was no bother of any kind this time from advice, orders or even suggestions. We marathoners ran or not in the time allotted to us on the ship and after we arrived in Amsterdam our training was entirely under our own supervision. This system was ideal. Had I but been free sixteen years previous at Stockholm, what a difference it would have made! Still had I won in 1912, I might have had an offer to turn pro that was tempting and thus have lost years of fun as an amateur runner and probably the extra windfall of money would be gone by now, anyhow.

The conditions under which this race was to be run would be the same as most Olympics in having a flat course with a run of thirteen miles out and back, but it would be different in that the climate of Holland is wet and cool. Before the race all competitors received a list of regulations. Among them I recall that: all suits must be clean, a shirt must be worn, there was to be no jumping in canals to cool off (the canals were very sluggish and used as fences between pastures. They were usually covered with green scum, which looked like cooked spinach). No refreshments were to be taken except at the regular stations about three miles apart, where they would have milk, water, tea, coffee, wine, bananas, hard boiled eggs, and anything else anyone left with the authorities beforehand. Later, a supplementary set of instructions was sent out and included one that no man was to jump in the river, either! Of course there were also the expected regulations about not hooking rides, leaving the course or interfering with other runners. Ordinarily any sane runner would naturally obey all the rules they sent out without reading them, except, perhaps the one about not removing his shirt. Surely, no one would want to jump in the canals! But being new to marathoning and very conscientious, the

Dutch didn't want to overlook anything. Fortunately no restrictions were placed on the number of strides or the number of breaths per minute!

As usual in an Olympic marathon there were seventy-five or eighty contestants representing about twenty-five nations. After we had gone several miles it became quite evident that a lot of the men were pretty good. I soon found myself in the rut, with no warm weather to thaw out my pep, racing with Germans, Dutch, English and others as well as Jimmie Henigan and Agee; with Ray, Michelson and many fast ones far ahead. I smiled reminiscently as I had an individual race with a German. Here was one of the "Huns" I had been conscripted to fight ten years ago. Now we were just racing for the fun of it. I wondered if he had watched me run when he was a boy at Coblenz. Anyhow it looked as though it would be a close struggle as to which of us would finish in the first thirty. Suddenly we came to a refreshment stand. Like a customer at a wayside booth he stopped and with arms akimbo carefully considered whether he'd have bananas or hardboiled eggs.

Finally I finished twenty-seventh, which is by far the worst I've ever done, yet the time was about two hours and fifty minutes and is nearly the same as that which got me a third at Paris four years before! Partly because of the cool weather and level course and a good deal because of the improvement in the speed of marathoners from all over the world, there were a lot of men able to do the Amsterdam race in splendid time. How widespread this marathoning ability has become is shown by the fact that the first five men came from five continents. El Oaufi, the first man, representing France, was from Morocco; the second man was from Chili; the third, a Jap; the fourth, a Finn; and fifth, our own Joie Ray. Michelson also did well, getting in the first seven or eight.

The biggest disappointment to me about this race was not that I finished in the rut, but that my suggestion for having all coaches abolished for marathoners at the

Olympic Games was lost, temporarily, at least. In 1932 they dug up someone for a marathon coach. Still, the Americans finished in the rut because the others happened to be better, but the committee was not so eager to abolish the idea of a coach in 1936 as they were to adopt him in 1932!

The rest of the team: Agee, Frick and Henigan were much further back than I. But all finished very close to three hours, which was really the best any Olympic marathon team had ever done for actual time.

Aside from the marathon in the varied high class competition at Amsterdam different things would stand out in different people's eyes, but the final of the four hundred meters was as thrilling as anything. Barbuti, of Syracuse, our hope, drew the inside lane. Some say this lane is not so good as the second, for all the distance-men have dug it up so much. However, it had been well rolled. Of course the start was staggered so that it looked as though Barbuti were handicapped. Around they sprinted and down the home stretch with the stadium rising in suspense. The finish was so close that no one but the judges knew who had won. But when the photographers began to take pictures of Barbuti we knew that America had won her only flat race at the 1928 Olympics!

Of course we looked around Amsterdam and its neighborhood. We were impressed by the apparent lack of poverty. There were no slums. Still the Dutch boys and girls, like most Europeans, liked to beg coins from the Americans. And the taxi drivers charged what the traffic would allow. We quickly learned to ask the price before getting in. It was strange to watch the thrifty Dutch collect tolls at bridges by reaching down for the coin with a wooden shoe hitched on a fishpole as motor boats taxied about the canals.

The many collections at church showed that the Dutch are good business people. I mentioned to Jimmie Henigan that we had three collections at our church service. He said, "That's nothing, we had five at ours!"

A week after the marathon a number of us went to Rotterdam for a post-games meet. There was the usual program of track and field events and a 12-mile race. There were representatives of several nations there and I expected several of them to do the twelve miles very fast. But it seemed just like being back home to have Jimmie Henigan win and myself get second. Afterwards, wishing to make the most of the meet, I ran in the 5000 meters. I found that I was somewhat in the rut, although not the worst. At first the Dutch fans began to razz me, but an announcer with a megaphone explained that I'd already run the twelve-mile race, where upon they gave me a great cheer. The fine line between the cheers and boos of any crowd is a thing to ponder!

That evening the Dutch at Rotterdam gave us a big banquet. There were lots of food, drinks, music and dancing. They'd eat or drink awhile, then jump up and all dance around the table, then sit down to fuel up some more. It was a hilarious occasion. The ice cream was served on a huge platter and was molded in the form of George Washington on a big white horse. Even one or two of the marathon team, who usually are the most abstemious on these trips, got a little too much wine. Outside of a little feud between some of us runners and a group of officials, the trip home was uneventful. We disliked the idea of giving up our room and there was a little "holding the fort" necessary. Funny how you remember things like that as part of an Olympic trip.

Throughout the winter of 1928-29 I realized that the old elasticity was not there. I did not improve with more training. I ran the forty-four miles from Providence to Boston again but instead of being a couple of miles ahead I was that far back of Karl Koski at the finish. Then I thought of passing up the B.A.A. as I figured the best I could do was two hours and forty-five minutes. However, I ran, and came in ninth in two hours and forty-three minutes.

During June 1929, I was invited out to Los Angeles to run in the Times Marathon. In the heat of that climate I felt very much like lying down under a palm tree and taking a siesta, but true to my habit of always finishing, I kept on. A Hopi Indian, Chauca, won in fair time and I was second, taking over three hours. There were a lot of other Hopis there and I noticed the sparkle of joy in their eyes that one of them had beaten me. (The great distance I came made me seem important to them.)

While en route out there, the train had a long wait at El Paso, Texas. So I went over to explore Juarez. Finding my time gone I came running back. The American guard at the boundary asked for my birth certificate. I hadn't brought one, but he just laughed and said, "All right, you're an American. No Mexican would run."

But the biggest evidence of my decreasing ability to run was delayed until 1932, when many considered that I had a chance of making the Olympic team again. With a cool day and a fast field I had to fight hard to get eighteenth. Then during the summer I was invited to the National Championship at Washington. With a hot day this time, all I could do was tenth. In this race I had a unique experience. While racing through the streets of the capital, some miles from the finish I asked a man, who had water, for a drink. He said what he had was spoken for, but he'd get me some. He cut across the park and met me on a parallel street with a drink. "Bah!" I spit it out "What's the matter with this water?" "I don't know," he replied, "I just dipped it up out of the lagoon."

Eight days later I was invited to run against Zabala, the new Olympic champion at Rockingham Park, N. H. As expected, content with his world honors, Zabala didn't bother even to finish. Michelson won, Johnny Semple was second and I was given third. McCune of Medford and his friends put up a big holler and claimed the officials had made a mistake and donated me one lap or a mile, so he should have been third. After getting home and catching my breath and reflecting on the various angles of the race I became convinced that McCune was right and that he should have been third. So the A.A.U. officials have donated me one mile to date by mistake. Should they ever make a mistake the other way I'll try to be easy on them.

Almost the only bright spot in my slipping career of 1932 was a third at the New England championship marathon from Boscawen to Manchester, N. H. on October 12th. But even here my time was over three hours, with Semple and Pasquale ahead of me.

While I got eighth in the B.A.A. in 1933, I was still slipping from placing among the first three, which is my ideal for a marathon. 1934 found me back in sixteenth place in the big marathon and apparently passing out of the picture. Then came 1935, which was my worst year of all. I was eighteenth in the Boston Marathon and just barely made it in three hours. The reason back of this bad year, aside from old age, was a lameness in one hip that no amount of osteopathy could cure that year, although it helped it a great deal. Unlike a sore knee, or a sore ankle or the calf of the leg, none of which seem to slow me up, a sore hip puts me back from fifteen minutes to a half hour.

In the Bunker Hill Marathon on June 17 from Lawrence to Charlestown, I was able to keep up with the leaders for about three miles, but from there on I could just plod through. Coming to a sign at about halfway which said: "Beginning measured mile," I timed myself with the watch I was carrying to the "End of measured mile." The time was six minutes and fifty seconds—just fifty seconds slow per mile. Charging up Bunker Hill, I could almost see the whites of Jimmie Henigan's eyes as he turned to see who was coming, but I couldn't catch him and so finished ninth which is a poor showing for a marathon with merely a local field.

On Labor Day, 1935, I was invited to Philadelphia for the first marathon of the Olympic Club. In this Philadelphia race some people seemed to expect me to do much better than was possible. One man urgently suggested that I change to the other side of the street. I snapped, "Who is running this race, anyhow?" He replied, "You ain't running." I'd like very much to have him for a judge in some of my walking races! Finally, I got twelfth in something like two hours and fifty minutes. Pat Dengis won this, and it was a remarkable performance after running a ten-mile race in Toronto two days before and then driving down the next day.

October 12th, as usual, I took in the Boscawen-Manchester Marathon. Way in the rut at the half-way point, I managed to creep up and gave Semple a hard fight for third, beating him on the home stretch in two hours and fifty-one minutes. I've always counted Semple one of the best of my many marathon friends, yet somehow I always like to race him especially, and count the race a partial success when I'm ahead of my friend.

My wife and I both went to the renewal of the Yonkers Marathon on Thanksgiving. They had advertised this as an Olympic try-out. This proved to be an exaggeration, for everyone had to prove his worth again in the spring. But there was a large entry, because of the publicity and excellent prizes. Without undue exertion I managed to be first or second for a couple of miles, doing perhaps a five minute and forty-five second mile. But my hopes didn't last long for I was back in twenty-eighth place at eighteen miles. Finally, I finished eleventh just back of the last good prize. Johnny Kelley won and was just two full mile laps ahead of me. There was just a speck of encouragement in the race for me, in that I did both the first and the last miles as fast as anyone. As the B.A.A. drew around again I realized that this was one of several times when I would have no show of winning. I even thought of passing it up to concentrate on the 50,000 meter walk for which I had been practicing. But as April 19th came during vacation time I just ran the race from habit, and eleven minutes better than the year before, finishing sixteenth. People along the B.A.A. course no longer expect me to win, and hence are not unduly urgent. They always give me a tremendous welcome everywhere. I wish I could store up some of the cheers to compensate for some of the knocks I'm sure to get before the next year!

Most of the runners are very glad that the B.A.A. marathon has survived the depression. It is well policed, and with officials who have been on the job since 1897, the management couldn't be any better. Still individuals will get in the way. During this last race a drunk got between me and the finish at Chestnut Hill and was bound that we should shake hands. I busted him on the chin, but skinned my knuckles on his thick beard. I didn't turn around to see how he made out, but I wonder if he still wants to shake hands with a competing marathoner.

After the marathon I concentrated my practice on the long walk. While perhaps harder on some muscles than running, this did not cause nearly so much nervous strain and I enjoyed it. In long road-walking races the only rule to distinguish walking from running is that you must have one foot touching the ground at all times. The N.E.A.A.U. generously voted to pay my way to the Olympic tryout at Cincinnati. In practice I "walked" the thirty-one miles in four hours and thirty minutes. Wishing to be of help, some of the athletic officials had me show them some of my "walking." They advised me to take it slow for the first half of the race to be sure I was walking and to save my energy. As they had voted me the funds for the trip I followed this advice, contrary to my judgment. It took more energy to go slow than fast and as soon as I started to speed up at the half-way point the judges warned me that I was running and I had to slow up to avoid being disqualified. Had I gone fast at the start it might have passed as walking and certainly I'd have removed a lot of the distance while fresh. Finally I finished fifteenth in five hours and fifty minutes. I expect to go in a lot more of these races in the future. What walking needs is an electric gadget, which will ring as you leave the ground! If every walker had one it would relieve the judges of guessing. But with all the walking I expect to do some more running.

An interesting angle of this slipping period has been the turning topsy-turvy of some convictions I once had about the best way to train for marathons. No longer does my success always depend on the amount of practice I do. Frequently, a rest and just a little practice causes me to make a better showing. No longer does the amount of sleep have much to do with how well I run. Often I do better on five, than eight hours rest. No longer does slow practice always produce the best race. Sometimes speed work causes me to do better. No longer can I criticize the man who likes his beer and his cigarettes while training. Some, even as old as I, seem to do almost as well without being abstainers. So the older I get, the less dogmatic and sure I become as to the best way for anyone else to get into physical condition. It is more than I can attend to, to know all the angles and changes necessary to be in the best shape myself. Not only are there individual differences, but the same individual has to change his method of training over a period of years, even as old people change their glasses!

Chapter 13
Some Victories In
My Old Age

Just as some days an old car runs fully as well as a new one, so now and then a marathoner between forty and fifty can beat all comers. Webster and Wyer, the Canadians, are good illustrations of this. Webster is nearly as old as I am, yet won the British Empire Games in 1934, and made the Canadian Olympic team in 1936. Wyer has been Canadian champion within a few years.

And I, also, have run some very good marathons since I was forty. There was a time when entries were received for the B.A.A. only between the ages of eighteen and forty, but the top limit has been removed and I won it in 1930 when I was nearly forty-two. In fact, I have won seven marathons open to all comers since I was forty. Four of these victories were in the good year of 1930. A description of these seven victories, with an attempt to explain how I could beat all competitors when so old, should be interesting.

On Labor Day, 1929, after rather a poor year, I accepted an invitation to run a full marathon in Halifax, Nova Scotia. I had a field of thirty or forty from all Eastern Canada to compete with. The race this time was on a hot day as contrasted to that in November, 1927, when it was so cold that I got chilled and finished walking in tenth place. But this time, with a hot day and a small field, I won in about two hours and fifty minutes. This victory is explained by the fact that the heat made it possible for two hours and fifty minutes to be the winning time. While I am writing this, seven years later, I can still do two hours and fifty minutes for a marathon, and in this time I might win as at Halifax or get twenty-seventh as at Amsterdam. It depends on the caliber of the field and whether or not it is hot enough to kill most of the others off.

The Canadians in this and other races were always very generous with traveling expenses and they also gave good prizes. This time they said they'd send a watch. Sure enough in about a week I received a Gruen watch from Cincinnati. At least they were not going to have any duty to pay! On several occasions as we came over the border the customs officers were a little curious about the silver cups. Once at the mention of tariff Jimmie Henigan simply said, "Well then, keep the cup," and they let him pass.

Right after this trip I got married and I heard continually from all sides that I should give up running. These people seemed to assume their superiority and my inferiority with their unsolicited advice for married happiness. Usually no reasons were given for my quitting the game, but I suppose they meant that it took too much time. However, even a married man needs some recreation and I can see no reason why I shouldn't take my fun in any way that pleases me most. Running has several advantages as a pastime. It is economical in cost of equipment and in the space required, and the time is optional; it is not dangerous to life or limb; and it usually improves health.

About this time I also changed my work and came to Keene Normal School[2] to teach and be the school printer.

---

[2] The Keene Normal School is now Keene State College.

On October 12 I ran so well in the Port Chester Marathon that Michelson, in good condition, was barely able to beat me the last mile. So married life and school teaching were showing no bad influence as yet.

That winter I practiced a good deal and felt so well that I was very confident of being up front in the big marathon in the spring, although most people didn't give me much chance after my ninth of the year before. However, the day was very warm and at the halfway point I was ahead of all except Oldag of Buffalo. I passed him before the hills and won as I pleased in two hours and thirty-four minutes.

That B.A.A. victory, however, was only the beginning of a very good year. Married life and the change from printing to a delightful situation at Keene, with some studying myself to keep my mind fresh and off running, was giving me an impetus. It is a phase of success at the game that I have not mentioned—that with me the greatest victories always come when I have something to occupy my mind strenuously. When I've had no time to think of running as the main object of life, I've done much better than when I've taken things easy mentally. My brain seems to need exercise as well as my body, but mental work is usually harder to begin than physical!

The month following the B.A.A. I went to Pawtucket to run in their marathon. With a trip to Los Angeles in mind for the next month, I ran conservatively and won in creditable time, but not so good but what Johnny Semple could break my record in a year or two. During this race I had my narrowest escape from serious accident. While running on the left-hand side of the road with traffic moving at about the same rate on the right, a car swung out of line suddenly and came bearing on me at forty miles per hour. I was the only thing in the way to prevent him from making a long gain around end. When about twenty-five yards away the driver spied me and decided not to run me down. With a screeching of brakes and a swerving into the ditch I was safe.

Then came the Los Angeles Times Marathon in which I had finished second the year before. As soon as I arrived some men at the club told me they thought I'd surely win because the Indian, Chauca, would no longer do what they said! "Why," they continued, "That blooming Indian even has a girl now!" Then I was almost sure I'd win, not because the Indian had a girl, but because of the presumption of those associated with him who set themselves on high to make the runner live artificially.

As good as the west coast is in most forms of sport, with their Rose Bowl victories and frequent intercollegiate track champions, they seldom have any good marathoners except the Indians. In this 1930 race I was soon in the lead with seven or eight Indians right on my heels and the rest far behind. I recalled the dime novels of my adolescence. How thrilling to have eight excited redskins running after me! These Indians had wanted a rule forbidding any water for contestants during the race, but I demurred saying I thought some water absolutely necessary under the hot sun at that distance. They cheerfully agreed to my wishes but I proved to be the only one near the front wanting any refreshments. Those Hopi Indians from the desert ran twenty-six miles in the heat with no water and no sweating either, so far as I could see.

Along about halfway a press car just barely bumped my heel. They were very sorry and showed their repentance by giving me water every quarter mile for the rest of the race. This surely helped me in the hot sun. They would just hand the water to me in a paper cup and I'd drink it or pour it on my head as I needed. A man in another car, seeing how I enjoyed the liquid, drove ahead, got a pail full and let me have it all over with the remark, "Hi, DeMar, I saw you run in Halifax." I wished he had stayed there instead of coming the four thousand miles to bother me. It took me three miles to squash all the water out of my shoes.

But with the water coming frequently from the press car, as I needed it, I kept up the pace shading ten miles per hour right through. Often on a hot day, one will "crack" or at least slow up his pace after fifteen or twenty miles. But I kept my stride right through and won in two hours and thirty-four minutes plus, about the same as at Boston and one-half hour better than the year before on the same course. This was one of the best marathons I ever ran in my life, considering the heat, and the record still stands for the course. Neither Fred Ward nor Whitey Michelson could break it in the next two years. So at the age of forty-two with refreshing things to occupy my mind and a "break" on physical condition, I could run very well at times.

The Keene Normal School had given me nine days to go clear across the continent and back. So I had the management of the race pay extra expenses to enable me to fly from Los Angeles to Kansas City and thus get back on time. This, the only airplane ride in my life, was worth running many miles for. But airplane riding has become so common to most people that when I proudly asked a lot of school children in a Vermont town far from the railroad how many had ever ridden in an airplane, over half said they had!

During the summer of 1930 I worked at Camp Zakelo in Maine. I had both to teach and produce printing, so I became tired, yet early in September on a very hot day, got fourth in Baltimore, being beaten by Agee, Wyer and Martak; then a week later I was third; at Hamilton, Ontario, being within three hundred yards of the winner.

About this time our first baby, Dorothy DeMar, came. Many people had hoped more than the parents that it would be a boy and a probable runner. However, already Dorothy acts like a runner, and maybe by the year 1948 will be another Hasenfus or a Stevens.

The year 1930 was to have one more marathon victory, that at Port Chester on October 12. At this place the prizes are always very fine, and now, being married, I had a good excuse to hasten away from the banquet and lots of speeches which tire one more than the race.

So 1930, with four marathon victories and a third and a fourth out of six starts, was one of my best years. And there was no fluke about it either, with a little more care I might have won all six races! For at Baltimore I had the lead until three miles from the finish, and at Hamilton I was on the same one-quarter mile lap as the winner. While most of these races were on hot days, which helped me by killing off my opponents, the Hamilton race was in the cool rain.

At the close of 1930 a committee of the A.A.U. recommended me as a candidate for the then new honor of being awarded the Sullivan medal for being the one who had done the most for amateur athletics during the year. A number of officials and newspapermen throughout the country vote on ten leading candidates. Some of the things they consider are: success in competition, number of years at the game, amateur attitude, sportsmanship, etc. That year Bobby Jones, still an amateur, got more votes than all the others together. And I was honored by getting the second most votes. A couple of times since, I have been one of the ten candidates for the medal.

The year 1931, with a fifth in the B.A.A. and a fourth at Port Chester, didn't bring any marathon victories. I rejoiced greatly at Jimmie Henigan's victory in the big race after trying for twenty years, and Dave Komonen won at Port Chester. In the latter race, Michelson, Henigan and I were delighted to come in 2nd, 3rd, and 4th. We had often finished together while junketing around Nova Scotia with lots of expenses and the good-will of the people because of our "fine sportsmanship and amateur spirit," as a Canadian official wrote. At that time, we began to call ourselves "the three musketeers" and years later finished 11th, 12th, and 13th in a fifteen-kilometer championship at Norwich, Connecticut.

After 1930, my next marathon victory did not come until 1933, when I was invited to Cleveland for the first marathon of the United Irish Societies. We ran from one side of the city right through the center of the lake metropolis and ended at Euclid Park. The race came on a scorching day. I had the lead at the halfway point and tore through the principal streets of Cleveland with two motor cops and sirens clearing the way. The Irish must have great influence out there to thus stall traffic and other business right in the middle of the afternoon. I was both amused and pleased to have authority precede me and clear the road before thousands of Ohioans. Many of them had not seen races before and hence were not so enthusiastic as in Boston or New York. However, they seemed to know me and several shouted something like "DeMar, the old fellow is pretty good yet." In all my career I've never felt prouder than this day in the lead with two sirens screeching passage.

Coming down the last few miles I was sure of winning, barring accident, but small boys on bikes always threatened to make one. Finally, I won in a little over three hours. Percy Wyer of Toronto, forty-eight years old, was second. Percy's friends let it be known that he could have beaten me only the officials led him on the wrong course. But they were mistaken. It happened in this way. At a point about eighteen miles from the start in some park the arrow on the course pointed one way and the officials, for some reason, steered all the runners, including Wyer and myself, over another route for a few miles. It was unfortunate that so excellent a race should have had this flaw. They might at least have taken down the sign. When the arrow says one way and the officials another, the only thing to do is to go as the officials say. Usually courses are fairly well marked with signs or guides. I only recall going wrong once in all my experience. That was a minor race and I got back on the course before the finish and no one knew the difference. Once, too, in a cross-country race at Franklin Park, Boston, they told us to go between the red and white flags, but that there were also some golf course flags and to use our own judgment on these I simply followed the leaders.

The year 1934, notwithstanding my sixteenth in the B.A.A., developed into a good year for marathoning. I had begun to experiment with some radical ideas of Hauser, Jackson, Bragg and others about diet. Their chief emphasis was to have an alkaline reaction in seventy-five percent of the food. This is found in fresh fruits and vegetables as contrasted to the acid of starches and meats. They also recommend plenty of vitamins and that foods be not over cooked. Hauser further advocates an elimination diet of one week living on just fresh fruits and vegetables, except potatoes and bananas (both starchy). I tried this limited diet for a week at a time several times during that summer and fall. It was surprising how much faster I could run after each of these weeks of self-denial. But I guess such things should be done only once or twice a year if one is working as hard as a marathoner does; for, while I got wonderful results up to cold weather with perhaps five partial fasts, something went wrong with my spine and hip in the early winter of 1934-35 and I've never been right since. So my experience points that some "elimination" is good but that it should never be over-done, especially in the winter. As I ordinarily use a lot of milk, which has calcium in it, and there is no milk in this diet, I suspect that a lack of calcium caused the trouble. During the summer, too, I got plenty of fresh leafy vegetables in which there was calcium.

One good effect of this alkaline diet has been greatly reduced dental bills. Some points of emphasis of these authorities mentioned above are interesting. For instance, they claim white sugar should not be used as its vital elements have been eliminated and it has such an affinity for iron that it must be refined in a copper, not an iron, kettle, hence it will draw the iron from one's system. They also joke about most breakfast foods with the life eliminated. They even claim that a few bugs in the oatmeal, as I once saw at St. Johns, are a very good sign, for many breakfast foods are so insipid that no self-respecting worm would go near them!

At any rate, my experiments this time did show results, as contrasted with those in 1911 under Dr. Kellogg, which made no difference. First, these alkaline fresh vegetable diets seemed to bring me better teeth and continue to do so. Second, they brought me three very fine marathons in the fall of 1934 and then the worst slump of my life, which is not over yet. So there is something to the diet theories; but if anyone is interested in experimenting he should be very careful, lest in doing things different from the majority, he becomes not better, but worse than the rest.

A description of these three successes, which were the result of experimenting in diet follows. When I went to Cleveland I felt so well that I knew I'd be near the front. The day came cool. Mel Porter and I ran close for half the race, then he pulled away, beating me by nearly a mile in two hours and thirty-one minutes. My time was two hours and thirty-seven minutes—nearly a half-hour better than the year before, when I won, and fast enough to win almost any marathon, except the B.A.A. or an Olympic!

October 12th, when the Boscawen-Manchester race came, I was so sure of my condition that I announced to everyone that I should win. Only three times in my career have I plainly said before a race that I'd win. These times were the 1924 B.A.A.; the 1927 Baltimore, and this one. Every time I have made good, but I nearly slipped this time and I'll have to be pretty good before I make another bold prophecy of victory.

That Manchester course is the full distance and may be a little long. It is over concrete roads and rolling hills.

The previous record was about two hours and forty-five minutes. I ran five miles in twenty-nine minutes and thirty seconds; ten in fifty-nine minutes and thirty seconds; and fifteen in one hour twenty-nine minutes thirty seconds. All the time Tarzan Brown, the Indian, was right with me. His handler kept bossing him and refusing to let him run ahead. He could have rolled up one half-mile lead early, but his boss said "not yet." The fact that there were two of them trying to run with one pair of legs gave me confidence that I should win and besides, I had said I was going to, so I continued to race hard with the Indian, who was very good indeed, even if he did have someone to spoil his concentration. At twenty miles, which we did just under two hours, his trainer began to urge Tarzan ahead. All he could get was one hundred yards lead at the most and I would close in frequently. Finally, at twenty-three miles I passed him for the last time. But Tarzan didn't fall back much and coming down the home stretch I didn't dare to risk turning to see how close he was. One cop would say he was thirty yards back and another one hundred fifty yards, so I wasn't sure of victory until I broke the tape. I won in two hours thirty-six minutes with Tarzan a few seconds back. We two were at least a mile ahead of any other time which had been made. I'm curious to see whether Kelly, Pawson or McMahon can break this record sometime. I consider this race at forty-six years of age one of the best of my life.

A few weeks later I ran in the Middle Atlantic Championship at Wilmington, Delaware. The course was long and winding and Mel Porter, who had beaten me by a mile at Cleveland, beat me this time by only a hundred yards, with Pat Dengis third.

So since I was forty and definitely slipping I have won seven full marathons, got second six times, and third four times; a total of seventeen times within the first three places. I'm wondering what I can do after I'm fifty!

Chapter 14
Teaching

Ever since I started to earn my living, I have enjoyed working with young people during such time as I could spare from my regular job. Even as far back as 1915 I thought of combining printing and teaching as a full time job. I dropped into a teachers' agency one noon in Boston. My enthusiasm was cut short when, with one glance, the man snapped, "If you want to teach school you must keep your hair combed." To be thus rudely told that the outside of the head was more important than the inside for teaching sent me back to the print shop, quite grateful for my independence as a mere compositor.

But along in the summer of 1929 as I was about to be married and realized I must be very sure of my income, I wondered if I couldn't do better as a teacher. During a minor depression in the spring of 1914, just before the war boom, several compositors were laid off. One of these laid off had gone into teaching and now Dick Barry was one of the best-paid and most successful teachers of printing in Boston.

Yes, I still must see what teaching had to offer, for although the depression had not yet begun, still I knew the printing business had not been booming for several years, and I could not afford to have short time. So I dropped into the Teacher's Exchange and asked them to find me a position as a teacher. They said I was too old to fit suddenly into a profession where the others had paid the price of years of experience and study and would be jealous of anyone butting in. But they said I might as well register and they would see what they could do.

In a few weeks I was in line for a position at a junior High School in Everett, teaching printing. But although the principal and superintendent wanted me, the school committee voted me down as inexperienced with discipline; and they had a lot of tough kids.

A little later Mr. Mason of Keene Normal School hired me to teach a little printing, do some myself, and anything else they might find. Pretty soon the men in the shop began advising me not to take this position, as the further away from a big city you went the harder you worked, and the less pay you got. The superintendent of the print shop even offered to raise my pay from forty-two dollars to forty-five dollars per week to stay. In this case I proved to have made a lucky choice, for the print shop failed within a year.

Keene let me come a week late, since I was getting married. About a week after I arrived the dean managed to find about a dozen students who wanted to learn a little something about printing. Although they only came two or three hours a week, most of the young people were bright enough so that they could soon do a lot of simple printing.

About a week later they also had me teach industrial history to a large class of girls. These girls were very industrious and some of them of superior intelligence, so I had to make my old brain almost creak to keep up, but after a few months I got used to it. The second half we were supposed to visit and study industries. After voting on which to go to, the class had a great time hiking around to mills, print shops, shoe factories, bakeries, etc. Keene has nearly sixty small industries, so it was easy to find interesting places to go. I kept this up for several years, getting the boy's division, also, the second year. But after four or five years they cut me down to just a few Trades and Industries boys in this subject. The students seemed to appreciate the trips a great deal, anyhow.

Several amusing incidents happened on these visits. Whenever we went to factories we listed among other things all the safety devices noticed, such as guards on fly wheels and pulleys, stop button, devices to pull the hands of operatives away from stamping machines, signs, rules, etc. After visiting a dairy farm one girl wanted to know if the ring in the bull's nose was a safety device!

But as these delightful years went past most of my teaching duties gradually faded away with the decreased enrollment and changes by the State Board of Education in reducing my Industrial History and Printing Classes. However, as a good printer, I found my printing work increasing all the time. And I kept working harder to hold on to the job lest I be unable to find another.

In the fall of 1932 I decided to go to Boston University and earn a Master's degree. The courses I wanted for that season came weekends so I advertised for transportation to Boston Friday afternoons at a price. A student going to Boston to see her mother agreed to take me down and back each week for two dollars. But after nine weeks, when practice-teaching began, this ride was no longer available. Then, unable to find anyone else going down regularly, I found I could walk and hitchhike the ninety miles in about four hours. At first I rather disliked to do this, as I felt ashamed to ask people for a ride, but soon got hardened to it the same as I did going around scantily clad when I first took up running years ago. However, as a teacher, I at least walked out of Keene before asking for a ride. Very often I didn't have to ask, since about a third of the people I rode with recognized and invited me.

So for two years I ran, walked and hitchhiked to Boston once a week, and my experiences and fun doing this made more of an impression on me than my studies. If my classes and work at Keene permitted, I allowed five hours for the trip down, otherwise four. In the two years I was never late to even one class and I had ninety miles to go! Usually I used the route through Fitchburg but now and then I went through Lowell and Nashua. Once with only forty-five minutes left I was dashing through Lowell hoping I wouldn't get off the route and watching for a ride. "Jump in," said someone, and sure enough I was going to make it, for he went sixty miles per hour towards Boston. He deposited me in Somerville and then on the trolley. I reached Professor Mahoney's class in "School and Society" just ten seconds before he rapped for attention.

The second year I went late Tuesday afternoons and evenings. The most fun came in getting home, after leaving classes at nine P.M. It would take nearly an hour by trolley to Arlington Heights and then long runs and walks and lifts now and then. I always got in before morning, except once, and usually about three A.M. Many people have the idea that there are no rides to be had after dark, but really there are more in proportion to the number of cars. As one man said, "Oh yes, I always pick people up at night, for what crook would walk in the dark when it's so easy to steal a car?"

The winter of 1933-34 happened to be a very cold one. One time I left Boston with the thermometer around zero and reached Keene with it thirty-one below zero. I could notice the drop as I journeyed north. At least there were no skunks out that evening. I had brushed one on a dark night in the early fall. He hadn't been offended, but I considered it a narrow escape from having to walk all the way home. On these cold nights my nose and face were the only parts liable to freeze and I'd keep rubbing them with snow as they got numb. Once a man let me out at the jail in Concord while he went to the left. Then seeing me walking along he turned around and came along side to warn me that I would never get a ride in the dark and might freeze to death. I just laughed and said that I always got a ride eventually and that I'd certainly freeze to death standing under the light. No, my system of hitchhiking was never to wait anywhere, because by keeping on the move I would eventually get there, and besides, cars might come out of a side road and be going my direction.

The fact that there was a hockey game at the Boston Garden on Tuesday nights was a big help to me. Once I got a ride near to Keene with someone who had been to the game, and often as far as Fitchburg. I was glad some people liked to watch sport well enough to journey fifty to one hundred miles after a day's work to see a game. One man taking me to Fitchburg gave me quite a lecture about an old fellow like myself walking nights. He was positive I'd get all tired out, and if not spry get hit by a truck. I assured him I was very tough. He was still sure I was liable to collapse. The next Tuesday night I happened to get a ride with the same man and then told him my name. He withdrew his advice about getting too tired.

As was to be expected in these all-night trips, I was questioned by the police several times. Once at Nashua in the rain, the patrol kept watching me as I walked through. They knew I was looking for a ride. Finally as I was leaving the city lights to stroll along the dark road towards Milford, they offered me a free night's bed, lest I collapse in the storm. I assured them of my ability to walk all night if necessary. That trip proved to be the one time I didn't get in before breakfast. I had to walk all the way from Wilton to Peterboro over Temple Mountain and a lot more besides.

Another time while walking through Concord, Massachusetts, I passed a couple of cops bawling out some spooners by the side of the road. They were full of fight for anything suspicious and stopped me. They wanted to know what I had in my brief case. I was glad to show them. They looked at the book The Educational Frontier and said in disgust, "Do you read that stuff?" "Just a little," I replied. After awhile they got my name and became very nice, wanting to know why I had not told them before. They asked about my prospects for April 19th and even tried to get me a ride with the spooners, who were headed in my direction. But these people didn't want a chaperone. My biggest time with the police came at Ayer. While walking past the road house just before crossing the railroad on the way to Fitchburg a cop stopped me. He was even more arrogant than an Olympic coach or official. "Where's your hat and coat?" he demanded. "Home, I can travel better without them." "Where are you going?" "Keene." "You live there?" "Yes." "Then you must know something about it. Who's the Chief-of-Police?" "Never had any trouble with him and don't know." "So you live in Keene and don't know the Chief-of-Police. Well, the main street, is that tarvia or concrete?" "As you leave the city it's tarvia, isn't it?" "I'm asking the questions! Have you any guns or knives?" "No." "Have you any money?" "Three or four dollars." I showed him the money. One is not a bum if he has two dollars in Massachusetts or fifty cents in New Hampshire, so I usually carry two dollars. "Have you anything to identify yourself?" my captor continued.

I showed him my folding book of checks. He saw the word "Keene" and relaxed. "Anything else you want to know?" I asked. "No," he said, "you can go, but you ought to be locked up—no hat and no coat!" Since he didn't ask me my name I didn't tell him.

On the whole I was sorry when my points were earned and I had my Master's degree in June, 1934; for the night walks had been invigorating and combined the mental stimulus of study made life very enjoyable.

Chapter 15
Conclusions

The question most often asked about running is whether or not it does any physical harm. I have never found any cases where it hurt anybody who is nearly normal. As to the best methods of getting into shape, that varies with individuals and with the same individuals as the years go by. Food, amount and kind of work, rest, habits of relaxation, whether to be an abstainer from liquor and tobacco or not, etc., all are questions it is impossible to answer dogmatically. Individuals differ. There is, however, one thing that I've always needed, and which everyone else that I've ever known has needed, and that is concentration, both just before and during the race. Without concentration no one can be ready to throw all he has into the race and no one can do everything he is capable of in the contest. What printer, what businessman, what editor, what schoolteacher wants distraction when he is working his hardest?

One thing that stands out in connection with my career and the publicity that came with the victories has been the desire of people to use my wins or anyone's wins to prove something they already believe in. Their reasoning is always deductive, never inductive. Hence, when I, a Sunday School teacher and an abstainer, won, they would use my victory to try to prove that no cigarettes, and no beer or other liquor were best, and that clean living was the only way to excel. On the other hand, when De Bruyn and Henigan won, each liking beer, that proved to some people, who wanted it, that beer made for great endurance. Very likely whether De Bruyn, Henigan or I used beer or not was about one to one thousand as compared to the necessity of having concentration. Of course all the ads endorsing this cigarette or that breakfast food are all deduction. If Jim Tuff eats corn-nuts and licks Jack Rut, then anyone who eats these nuts can lick anyone he chooses!

Dr. Kellogg's "experiment" with me seemed like propaganda for his fad. If he wanted to find out something he should have found two runners who were no good and then compared the improvement of the one using his calories over the other who ate anything he wanted.

Another question that might arise is about amateurs and professionals. Lots of people ask, "Why haven't you turned professional and made a lot of money?" One answer is simply because I never had a chance. I've had several opportunities to collect generous windfalls by "expenses" as an amateur, but only one offer to turn professional. That offer was not for ten thousand dollars nor one-thousand dollars, but just for two hundred dollars, to appear several times a day for a week at a theatre. That was right after the 1927 B.A.A. win and I was getting over forty dollars per week with occasionally a little extra, and it would have taken me three or four days to find another job, if I threw that one up to make the two hundred dollars, besides never being able to run any more important races. Being barred from the good races if not in the Amateur Union, is one of the biggest reasons why most of us prefer to stay "amateur" unless there is something worth while as a professional. The A.A.U. controls all the important running contests so it is a good policy to get along with them. Whether this body is doing any service by maintaining this control or whether it would be better to put the whole business on a dollar and cents basis is a question.

On the side of out-and-out professionalism is the argument that with high-class athletes, the world over there are no absolute amateurs. Of course in getting their expenses for trips any mistake will be in the amateur's favor, and there are apt to be gifts, both direct and indirect. The A.A.U. might just as well try to stop the tide from coming in by dipping and throwing pails of water out to sea, as to occasionally fire an athlete for getting a little "chicken feed."

On the side of amateurism is the big argument that it tones things down so that money does not play the important role that it would in out-and-out professionalism. As said before, the "amateurs" are relatively amateur, and with most of them the tendency to professionalism is not great. I've always maintained that amateur running is the fairest thing in the world. Aside from a few mistakes in counting the laps, the officials of all types and the runners, too, have always been so fair that with my twenty-seven years of competition I'd have hard work to recall even a couple of incidents that were otherwise.

Is there any way to improve the present system of marking the line between amateurs and professionals by whether they belong to the A.A.U. or not? I have no suggestions to make. This way is all right when one understands it, but is a little hard for the conscientious youth who takes everything literally. To illustrate this, I have in mind two young runners. One, brought up in a conscientious church home, said: "Mr. DeMar, I don't understand this amateur business, there's so and so, a great athlete. He does no work all summer, yet he is getting a good living." I replied, "No one fully understands it." But in delightful contrast to this stubborn literalist was a fresh kid with few inhibitions, who made good at the game quickly. He laughed and said, "Clarence

I like this amateur running. I can go like the dickens for five dollars!"

I might add that on the whole, runners are relatively better amateurs than boxers, for instance. Once, in speaking to a Lion's Club in a certain city, when I mentioned my opinion of amateurism vs. professionalism, with the necessity for elasticity in the interpretation of the rules a jeweler said, "I know something about that, too. When they had the boxing tournament here, I furnished all the prizes with the understanding that if any boxer wanted his money back I'd return it. All the prizes came back, so I had no permanent sales."

But while I have no suggestions for settling the amateur question, I have several for making Olympic trips of greater enjoyment and achievement. What a privilege it is to be selected from one hundred twenty-five million to compete against the best in the world. To reach a point good enough for this, one must work and pay attention; he must try to keep his indulgences not at zero, for all humans have failings, but at the lowest point that he knows will bring him best results; he must be quick to change his plan of training if what *was* good is not now producing results. And if after he has done all this, how much an anticlimax it is to find he is caught in the net of the authorities.

I am not discussing whether or not we need coaches or trainers, for most athletes in high school or college. I do not know much about any sport except distance running. I suspect coaches are a help to over half the cross-country squad in educational institutions. However, if anyone is outstanding enough to represent the United States in international competition I believe he has outgrown any need for overseers, especially so far as distance-running is concerned. Any idea that a man who is used as a puppet by a group of authorities can become a world-beater, is absurd. Just suppose, for instance, that each marathon runner raised his own funds to enter an international distance race, and went as he pleased, does anyone think that the first American would be eighteenth?

I don't know whether this would be the best way or not. I do know that it would at least eliminate the feeling of being rushed, of being bluffed, and would give each individual the proper tone and invigorating determination necessary for running a good distance race.

The power to achieve, to regulate one's life with regard to self-indulgence, or abstinence, comes from within. Any superimposed authority over things like this, shows as much sense as commanding the sun and moon stand still. There are many angles for individuals to work out in order to become champions. When prospective victors are selected, their methods must be as varied as the ideals and habits of the group. The American team is selected fairly. The Olympic Committee has done well with its collection of funds. But this end of their work has over-emphasized its importance in the making of a successful Olympic team. I have had my fun at running, and have learned a lot from it, but anything I can do for the good of future runners will be not so much in giving them my experiences, as in helping them to keep their independence as competitors, and to enter international competition, if they are chosen, with the feeling that their independence is still unhampered.

At the age of forty-nine I can truly say that, aside from Olympic junkets, the game has been worth it. Some people are born writers, that is, they may be good or bad writers, but they were born with something that makes them want to write. Just so some people are born competitors, and need the stimulus of athletic competition. These people may have started out as baseball players, and in later years transferred their efforts to golf. In my case I happened to stick to one sport. I still enjoy the long grind of the marathon.

Clarence H. DeMar

Keene, N. H. 1937

DeMar enjoying a visit at work with children
Charles, Dorothy and Robert (c. 1941)

Afterword:
Beyond 1937

Upon finishing his autobiography in 1937, which was first published that year by Stephen Daye Press in Brattleboro, Vermont, Clarence reportedly ran 20 miles from Keene, New Hampshire to Brattleboro, signed the contract, then turned around and ran the 20 miles back home to Keene! He continued to run for the rest of his life.

You may recall the following quote, which Clarence wrote in his autobiography at the age of 49:

> *"Since I was forty, and definitely slipping, I have won seven full marathons, got second six times, and third four times; a total of seventeen times within the first three places. I'm wondering what I can do after I'm fifty!"*

You might be wondering… *what did he do in his older years?*

DeMar officially completed the Boston Marathon a total of 33 times over the course of his legendary 48-year running career. At age 50 he was still among the top 20 Boston finishers. His marathon time never exceeded three hours until age 57. In 1954 DeMar ran his last Boston Marathon at age 65, finishing in 3:58:34. Completing over 1000 races, DeMar ran competitively until age 69 when he finished a 15k in Bath, Maine shortly before passing away.

Clarence and his wife Margaret had five children-Dorothy, Robert, Charles, and twin girls Barbara and Betty. The family continued to live in Keene, NH until 1943 when they relocated to the town of Reading, Massachusetts, approximately 12 miles north of Boston. Their farmhouse, which once overlooked the DeMar's rural 16-acre farm, still stands on Forest Street today, which has since developed into a suburban neighborhood. Tragedy struck the DeMar family shortly after the move when their youngest son Charles died of rheumatic fever. Their oldest son Robert was subsequently diagnosed with polio, although he eventually overcame the illness as a teenager.

While living in Reading, Clarence worked the nightshift in Boston as a proofreader for the Boston Herald Traveler newspaper. Locals still recall DeMar commuting the 12 miles each way by foot, rarely ever accepting a lift. He would also jog the 12 miles home from the Boston Marathon finish line each April, declining a ride home even in his 60s.

Hailed as one of the greatest distance runners of all time, Clarence, the person, is still remembered by those who knew him personally.

"He was highly intellectual," says Virginia Adams, who grew up with Mr. DeMar's twin daughters in Reading. "He'd name his cows after Greek gods and goddesses and would often bring up various topics of world affairs at the dinner table, which was very unusual for a working-class family at that time.

"We always knew where he was, because he was always talking to himself," Virginia recalls of his quirky personality. "He was just very unusual. I remember one time on the farm, in particular, Mr.

DeMar was standing over a hot fire during the summertime in his coveralls. 'You want some?' he asked. As we looked closer we noticed he was holding a squirrel on a stick and roasting it over the fire!" Virginia and the DeMar girls politely declined the offer.

Despite Clarence's reputation for having a cold and unfriendly personality as a runner (likely a result of the event he described in Chapter 12), the DeMars were known to be quite friendly and welcoming to those who knew them personally. The house was a favorite among local children and adults on Halloween thanks to his wife Margaret, who would hand out slices of pumpkin pie rather than candy. The DeMars were also known for allowing neighborhood children to board their horses on the farm.

On June 11, 1958 Clarence DeMar died at the age of 70 having succumbed to colon cancer. Dying just weeks after finishing 14th in a 15k road race, he ran right up until his final days. A doctor was claimed to have yelled at Clarence just a few days before his passing, upon walking into his hospital room to find Clarence jogging in place.

Clarence, the man who cared little for trophies, money or fame, took great pride in the fact that he finished nearly 100 marathons and over 1000 races without ever quitting before crossing the finish line. He was never one to give up... right up to his final days.

"Clarence crawled into the backyard and planted a garden," his wife Margaret recalled of his last day of life. "He simply refused to give up."

A postmortem cardiac examination of DeMar's body revealed that his arteries were two to three times larger in diameter than those of the average human's. This examination, which was performed by the famous Dr. Paul Dudley White, also debunked the early 20th century myth that distance running caused injury to the heart. Dr. White found that DeMar's heart, while enlarged, was normal and uninjured. An enlarged, though normal looking heart (now known as athletic heart syndrome) was found to be a healthy result of constant cardiovascular training. It is likely that this was the cause of a misdiagnosis of a heart murmur prior to DeMar's first marathon, though DeMar joked that his doctor must have accidentally been listening to his own heart, since the doctor died shortly after!

Since his death in 1958 Clarence DeMar has been honored on several occasions through memorial dedications as well as races held in his name. The Clarence DeMar Marathon has taken place annually in Keene, New Hampshire since 1978. A granite finish line marker for the race was dedicated in DeMar's honor in 2014. The Clarence DeMar 5k has been held annually since 1983 in South Hero, Vermont, where DeMar worked as a fruit farmer at the age of 16. The city of Melrose, MA dedicated a granite memorial to both Clarence DeMar & Bill Rodgers, both of whom were Melrose residents during each of their respective running careers. In 2000 Clarence DeMar was inducted into the National Distance Running Hall of Fame, and in 2011 was inducted into the USA's National Track & Field Hall of Fame.

More than one hundred years since winning his first marathon in 1911, Clarence DeMar still holds several unbroken records and is known as one of the greatest distance runners of all-time.

Clarence DeMar (1888-1958)

Clarence DeMar's
Boston Marathon Stats

Year	Place	Time	Age
1910	2	2:29:52	21
1911	1	2:21:39	22
1917	3	2:31:05	28
1922	1	2:18:10	33
1923	1	2:23:47	34
1924	1	2:29:40	35
1925	2	2:39:34	36
1926	3	2:32:15	37
1927	1	2:40:22	38
1928	1	2:37:07	39
1929	9	2:43:47	40
1930	1	2:34:48	41
1931	5	2:55:46	42
1932	18	2:46:15	43
1933	8	2:43:18	44
1934	16	2:56:52	45
1935	18	2:58:27	46
1936	16	2:49:08	47
1937	14	2:53:00	48
1938	7	2:43:30	49
1939	30	2:51:12	50
1940	27	2:55:32	51
1941	20	3:05:37	52
1942	24	2:58:14	53
1943	17	2:57:58	54
1946	32	3:09:55	57
1947	65	NA	58
1948	51	3:37:25	59
1949	49	3:28:42	60
1950	34	3:28:13	61
1951	66	NA	62
1953	81	NA	64
1954	79	3:58:34	65

CLARENCE
DEMAR
MARATHON
HALF MARATHON

Keene, New Hampshire

Every autumn hundreds of runners make the pilgrimage to Keene, New Hampshire, where Clarence DeMar lived and trained during the height of his legendary running career. This quaint New England town is host to the annual **Clarence DeMar Marathon & Half Marathon**, one of the oldest marathons in the United States.

The event takes place every year in the beautiful and scenic Monadnock Region of New England during the early fall foliage season. This fast marathon course includes gentle rolling hills and runs point-to-point from the village of Gilsum, over the Surry Mountain Dam and into the center of Keene. The finish line at the historic Appian Way of Keene State College is just steps from where Clarence DeMar once lived. The race is a Boston qualifier and a USATF-certified course. The second longest continuous running marathon in New England, it is just second to the Boston Marathon. The race is limited to 600 participants because of the rural nature of the roads and limits posed by nearby villages.

Clarence DeMar won the Boston Marathon seven times- a record that has yet to be broken. His first came at age 22 and his last win at age 41, another Boston record. He completed the Boston Marathon 32 times between the years of 1910 and 1954 in addition to representing Team U.S.A. at the Olympics in 1912, 1924 and 1928, winning bronze in 1924 in Paris.

159

During the 1920s and 30s Clarence taught industrial arts at the Keene Normal School, now Keene State College, in addition to coaching cross country and track. On weekends, DeMar, a Harvard graduate, would hitchhike and jog back and forth between Keene and Boston, a distance of over 80 miles each way, while earning his Master's Degree from Boston University.

Thanks to the strong relationship Clarence built with the school and the community, Keene State College has always played an integral role in supporting the Clarence DeMar Marathon on race day, providing space and facilities for runners to use. The City of Keene recognizes The Clarence DeMar Marathon as an official "Community Event".

In 2014 Keene dedicated a granite memorial post to DeMar at the finish line of the race. His daughter Betty, who has run the half marathon multiple times, was present for the unveiling of the memorial. Several of DeMar's family members have joined the races over the years including his grandchildren and great-grandchildren.

"We work very hard to honor the legacy of Clarence and his endurance accomplishments," says Alan Stroshine, the Clarence DeMar Race Director. In honor of DeMar's legacy as an endurance athlete and community philanthropist, the race has become a platform for a number of local wellness programs. One event includes the "Kids DeMar Marathon Program". More than 35 elementary schools and 1,200 kids participate in running or walking clubs at school and log 25 miles over the course of the summer. They complete their "marathon" on race day by running the final 1.2 miles of the marathon course. Parents are welcome and encouraged to walk or run the final 1.2 with their children, and the 25 miles beforehand, just like their kids.

The event hosts a similar program for the over 70 crowd- the "DeMar Super Seniors". These individuals follow a similar 25-mile program designed to keep them active and motivated before finishing the final 1.2 on race day.

The Clarence DeMar Marathon has also partnered with the local newspaper and medical center to promote the "13 in 13" program. "13 in 13" is a specially designed training program for beginner or intermediate runners, which includes guidance and coaching. These runners get together every Saturday for a "long run" to support and learn from each other. In 13 weeks, they are ready to start and finish their first half marathon together.

The "Follow ME" Sneaker program is another community wellness program involved in the DeMar Marathon. "ME" stands for Moving Everyday. As a part of this program, a brand new pair of New Balance sneakers is delivered to every 2nd grader in Cheshire County, New Hampshire. More than 800 pairs of sneakers were delivered in 2016 to help encourage kids to move everyday. The sneakers also come with a new pair of socks, family passes to the Keene YMCA and family passes to four summer collegiate baseball games in Keene.

Regardless of age or running experience, participants of the Clarence DeMar Marathon find a welcoming and well-organized community event full of supportive volunteers and spectators. The races truly embody the spirit of the legend himself, Mr. Clarence "DeMarathon" DeMar.

For more information on the Clarence DeMar Marathon & Half Marathon visit **www.ClarenceDemar.com**

"This is a small race in a gorgeous part of New England. It is extremely well organized, designed for runners. It is special because of the heritage and the man it honors, the volunteers and organizers LOVE their race, and it features the beauty of New Hampshire."
-2015 Clarence DeMar Marathoner

"The personal touches of the marathon were evident throughout. I particularly appreciated the welcome we received from the race director upon arrival at the start. The finish was also well organized and exciting with very personal recognition from the race announcer. I cannot recommend this race highly enough."
-2015 Clarence DeMar Half-Marathoner

"The first 15-16 miles or so are absolutely beautiful New England countryside. The race is extremely well organized, and most everyone involved with the race was positive and friendly. No crazy crowds or hassles!"
-2014 Clarence DeMar Marathoner

Photo Courtesy of Alan Stroshine

163